TABLE OF CONTENTS

TYPE 2 DIABETES MELLITUS (190 Q&A)

Etiopathogenesis (15) 11

1) What are the top 3 countries in the number of people with diabetes? 11
2) What is the pathophysiology of type 2 DM? 11
3) How does type 2 DM develop? 12
4) What is the role of beta-cell dysfunction in the pathophysiology of type 2 DM? 12
5) How does obesity affect the risk of developing type 2 diabetes mellitus (DM)? 12
6) What two factors must be present for type 2 DM to occur? 13
7) How does insulin resistance affect glucose tolerance in type 2 DM? 13
8) How does insulin resistance affect lipid accumulation and how is it managed? 13
9) What are the etiologic factors of type 2 DM? 13
10) What are the major risk factors for type 2 diabetes mellitus (DM)? 13
11) What is the rate of progression from IGT to overt diabetes? 15
12) What genes are associated with an increased risk of type 2 DM? 16
13) What genes are associated with maturity onset diabetes of youth (MODY)? 16
14) What are the causes of secondary diabetes? 16
15) What causes metabolic syndrome (syndrome X)? 17

Clinical features (5) 17

1) What symptoms suggest DM? 17
2) What are the symptoms of catabolism? 18
3) How will you take a focused history in a patient with established type 2 DM? 18
   A focused diabetes history should also include the following questions: 18
   As circumstances dictate, additional questions may be warranted, as follows: 19
4) What findings should be noted during foot exams for type 2 diabetes mellitus (DM)? 20
5) What are the indications for diabetes screening in asymptomatic adults? 21

Diagnosis (24) 22

1) What are the ADA diagnostic criteria for type 2 DM? 22
2) What is stress hyperglycemia? 22
3) What conditions can interfere with FPG test results 22
4) What conditions can interfere with HbA1c test results? 23
5) How is prediabetes defined? 23
6) What tests are needed to confirm a diagnosis of DM if unequivocal hyperglycemia is absent? 24
7) What additional testing is required if 2 different test results are discordant for DM diagnosis? 24
8) What are the criteria for screening for type 2 diabetes or prediabetes in asymptomatic adults? 25

9) What testing should be performed in an asymptomatic patient with random serum glucose level that suggests DM (>140 mg/dL)? 26
10) What HbA1c levels are considered diagnostic for prediabetes and diabetes mellitus (DM)? 26
11) What HbA1c levels are predictive of myocardial infarction risk? 26
12) What timespan does glycated hemoglobin measurements reflect? 26
13) How does a serum glucose measurement compare to a plasma glucose measurement in DM? 26
14) How are capillary whole blood measurements used in the diagnosis of DM? 26
15) What are the WHO diagnostic criteria for impaired glucose tolerance? 27
16) How is type 2 DM different from type 1 DM? 27
17) What are the clinical features that suggest type 1 diabetes? 27
18) How will you differentiate type 2 from type 1 DM? 28
19) What is the role of C-peptide levels in differentiating type 1 and type 2 DM? 29
20) What is "latent autoimmune diabetes in adults"? 29
21) How is latent autoimmune diabetes of adults (LADA) differentiated from type 2 DM? 29
22) Are autoantibodies useful in differentiating type 1 and type 2 DM? 30
23) What testing is done in the ED for all patients with diabetes mellitus (DM)? 30
24) How is metabolic syndrome (also called syndrome X) diagnosed? 30

Treatment (15) 31

1) What are the main goals of treatment for type 2 diabetes mellitus (DM)? 31
2) What are the guidelines for the initial management of type 2 DM? 31
3) What is medical nutrition therapy (MNT) for people with diabetes? 32
4) How effective is aggressive dietary modification in type 2 DM? 32
5) What is the role of weight loss in type 2 diabetes treatment? 33
6) How should diet be managed in patients with type 2 DM? 33
7) What are the 5 components of medical nutrition therapy (MNT) in DM? 33
8) What are the benefits of physical activity in type 2 DM? 34
9) When is cardiovascular evaluation needed prior to beginning a significant exercise regimen? 34
10) How are glycemic management decisions made for type 2 DM? 34
11) What are the guidelines on the antidiabetic drug therapy in type 2DM? 35
12) What are the drugs commonly used in the treatment of type 2 DM? 35
13) What is the initial treatment for asymptomatic patients with type 2 diabetes? 38
14) What is the initial treatment for symptomatic patients with type 2 DM? 38
15) How will you manage patients with severe hyperglycemia without ketonuria or weight loss? 39

Metformin (12) 40

1) What are the benefits of metformin use in the treatment of type 2 DM? 40
2) What are the beneficial actions of metformin in the treatment of type 2 DM? 40
3) Why is metformin the preferred initial therapy? 40
4) What are the most common side effects of metformin? 41
5) How do you titrate the dose of metformin? 41
6) What is the effect of metformin on vitamin B12 metabolism? 41
7) Can you use metformin if the serum creatinine level is 1.5 mg/dL? 41
8) What are the contraindications for metformin? 42
9) What are the recommendations for the addition of other oral drugs to metformin glycemic control? 43
10) What is the indication for dual-drug therapy in the treatment of type 2 DM? 43
11) If 2 drugs are unsuccessful, what options for triple-drug therapy are available for type 2 DM? 43
12) A patient has persistent hyperglycemia even after metformin 2g daily and lifestyle intervention. What is the next drug to be added? 44

Sulfonylureas (6) 44

1) Which oral agent has the greatest efficacy for glycemic lowering? 44
2) What is the mechanism of action of sulfonylureas? 44
3) By what percentage does sulfonylureas reduce HbA1c? 44
4) Which are the sulfonylureas with a shorter duration of action? 44
5) How should sulfonylureas be used in the treatment of type 2 DM? 45
6) What is the most common side effect of sulfonylureas? 45

GLP-1 agonists (12) 45

1) What are the beneficial actions of glucagon-like peptide-1 (GLP-1) agonists in type 2 DM? ... 45
2) What are the indications for using GLP-1 receptor agonists? 46
3) What is the glycemic efficacy of GLP-1 receptor agonists? 47
4) Which are the injectable GLP-1 agonists? 47
5) Which are the long-acting GLP-1 receptor agonists that can be given once weekly injections? 47
6) Which glucagon like peptide-1 (GLP-1) agonist can be given orally in type 2 DM? 47
7) How is exenatide given in type 2 DM? 47
8) What are the benefits of adding exenatide to insulin glargine in type 2 DM? 48
9) What are the benefits of combination therapy with GLP-1 receptor agonists and DPP-4 inhibitors? 48
10) What is the role of liraglutide in the treatment of type 2 DM? 48
11) What are the side effects of GLP-1 receptor agonists? 49
12) What precautions should be taken before giving GLP-1 receptor agonists? 49

Dipeptidyl peptidase 4 (DPP-4) inhibitors (3) 49
1) Which are the DPP-4 inhibitors available for the treatment of type 2 diabetes? 49
2) What is the role of dipeptidyl peptidase IV inhibitors (DPP-4 inhibitors) in the treatment of type 2 DM? 49
3) What are the benefits of linagliptin in the treatment of type 2 DM? 50

SGLT-2 inhibitors (11) 50
1) How do sodium-glucose transporter-2 inhibitors act? 50
2) What is the glycemic efficacy of SGLT2 inhibitors? 51
3) What is the role of SGLT2 inhibitors in the treatment of type 2 DM? 51
4) What is the role of canagliflozin in the treatment of type 2 DM? 52
5) What are the indications for dapagliflozin in the treatment of type 2 DM? 52
6) What are the indications for empagliflozin in the treatment of type 2 DM? 52
7) Which SGLT2 inhibitor is preferred in a patient with type 2 diabetes and a prior history of atherosclerotic cardiovascular disease? 53
8) Which SGLT2 inhibitor is preferred in a patient with type 2 diabetes and heart failure or kidney disease? 53
9) What are the adverse effects of SGLT2 inhibitors? 53
10) What are the contraindications for SGLT2 inhibitors? 54
11) How should a patient be evaluated prior to starting an SGLT2 inhibitor? 54

Meglitinides (4) 55
1) What are meglitinides? 55
2) What is the mechanism of action of meglitinides? 55
3) How should meglitinides be used to treat type 2 diabetes mellitus (DM)? 55
4) Can repaglinide be used in patients with chronic kidney disease? 56

Alpha-glucosidase inhibitors (1) 56
1) What is the role of alpha-glucosidase inhibitors in the treatment of type 2 DM? 56

Thiazolidinediones (6) 56
1) What is the mechanism of action of thiazolidinediones? 56
2) How should TZDs be used in the treatment of type 2 DM? 57
3) How effective are thiazolidinediones in the treatment of type 2 DM? 57
4) What are the adverse effects of thiazolidinediones to treat type 2 DM? 57
5) What are the contraindications for thiazolidinedione use? 58
6) Can thiazolidinediones be used for diabetes prevention? 58

Insulins (23) 59
1) Which are the commonly used insulin preparations? 59
2) When is insulin indicated as initial therapy in type 2 DM? 61
    1. Severe hyperglycemia on presentation 61
    2. Difficulty distinguishing type of diabetes 61

       3. Pancreatic insufficiency 61

       4. To eliminate glucotoxicity..61

   3) When is Insulin always indicated?..62

   4) Which are the rapid acting insulins?...62

   5) Which are the short-acting insulins? 63

   6) Which are the intermediate-acting insulins?..63

   7) Which are long-acting insulins? 63

   8) What is the role of long-acting insulins in the treatment of type 2 DM? 64

   9) Which insulin is preferred for initial treatment? 65

   10) What is the initial dose for basal insulin? 65

   11) When is basal insulin best given? 65

   12) Which basal insulin has the best glycemic efficacy?...66

   13) Is basal insulin alone adequate for glycemic management in type 2 DM?....................66

   14) How will you manage persistent fasting hyperglycemia?...66

   15) When is pre-meal insulin added to basal insulin? 66

   16) Which is the best prandial (related to a meal) insulin for type 2 diabetes?..................66

   17) Which is most effective in lowering postprandial glucose in type 2 DM? 67

   18) What is the role of insulin aspart/Fiasp in the treatment of type 2 DM?......................67

   19) Where is the preferred site for administration of insulin injections in type 2 DM?.............68

   20) What are the disadvantages of insulin therapy? 68

   21) Is combining oral hypoglycemic drug and insulin useful? 68

   22) A type 2 diabetic obese patient has persistent elevation in A1C with FBG in target range. How will you manage? 68

   23) What is the indication for pramlintide in the treatment of type 1 or type 2 diabetes?.......69

Practice points (26) 69

   1) What is the HbA1c target in type 2 DM? 69

   2) What are the desired goals of glucose values in type 2 DM? 70

   3) How should blood glucose levels be managed in type 2 DM? 70

   4) When will you start initial pharmacologic therapy? 71

   5) How will you make the choice of initial drug therapy? 71

   6) What is the easiest way to correct fasting hyperglycemia in type 2 DM?...........................71

   7) A patient on basal insulin has raised pre-lunch glucose with HbA1c 8%. How will you correct it? 72

   8) A patient on basal insulin has raised pre-dinner glucose with HbA1c 8%. How will you correct it? 72

   9) A patient on basal insulin has raised pre-bed glucose with HbA1c 8%. How will you correct it? 72

   10) How do you adjust the pre-meal insulin dose? 72

   11) What are the advantages and disadvantages of pre-mixed insulin?.............................73

12) What is the specific glucose value that defines hypoglycemia? 73
13) Which are the antidiabetic drugs that do not usually cause hypoglycemia? 73
14) What is pseudohypoglycemia? 74
15) How will you manage recurrent daytime hypoglycemia? 74
16) How will you manage recurrent episodes of nocturnal hypoglycemia? 75
17) What is the dawn phenomenon in type 2 DM? 75
18) What is the efficacy of intensive therapy for type 2 DM? 75
19) What is the treatment for diabetes mellitus in the ED when the type is unknown? 76
20) A 50-year-old male has fasting plasma glucose 280 mg/dL, random glucose 360 mg/dL, glycated hemoglobin 9.5 percent but without ketonuria or unintentional weight loss. What is the preferred initial therapy? 76
21) Which drug is preferred in patients with established cardiovascular disease? 76
22) Which drug is preferred in patients with established kidney disease? 77
23) Which drug is preferred in a patient with nondialysis chronic kidney disease stage 4 (eg, eGFR <30 mL/min/1.73 m2)? 77
24) A diabetic patient with A1C levels of 9% was put on metformin. After 6 months his A1C level is 10%. He cannot tolerate metformin anymore. Which antidiabetic drug would you use? ... 78
25) A diabetic patient with A1C levels of 9% was put on metformin. After 6 months his A1C level is 8.5%. He cannot tolerate metformin anymore. Which antidiabetic drug would you use? .. 78
26) How does type 2 diabetes affect morbidity and mortality in COVID-19? 79

Chronic complications and their prevention (27) 79

1) What factors influence the prognosis of type 2 DM? 79
2) What are the guidelines for monitoring complications in type 2 DM? 79
3) Which interventions may help prevent or limit the complications of DM? 79
4) How do the complications differ by type of DM? 80
5) What are the common vascular complications of type 2 DM? 80
6) What is the effect of glycemic control on the microvascular vascular complications in type 2 DM? 80
7) What is the effect of glycemic control on the macrovascular vascular complications in type 2 DM? 80
8) What is the most effective approach for prevention of macrovascular complications in type 2 DM? 81
9) What is the risk of coronary heart disease in adults with type 2 DM? 81
10) When does cardiovascular risk increase in type 2 DM? 81
11) Which lipid abnormalities contribute to cardiovascular risk in type 2 DM? 81
12) What are the guidelines for the use of statins in type 2 DM? 82
13) What are the guidelines on cardiovascular disease management and prevention in patients with diabetes or prediabetes? 83
14) What blood pressure goals are recommended for type 2 DM? 83
15) Which antihypertensive medications are recommended for type 2 DM? 84

16) When and how should screening for microalbuminuria be performed in patients with type 2 DM? 84

17) What does microalbuminuria indicate in type 2 DM and how does it differ from type 1 DM? 84

18) What are the ophthalmologic complications of type 2 DM?....................................85

19) What are the treatment options for neuropathy in type 2 diabetes mellitus (DM)?..........85

20) How does autonomic neuropathy manifest in type 2 DM?.....................................86

21) What are the acute-onset mononeuropathies caused by type 2 DM?............................86

22) What are the treatment options for gastroparesis in type 2 DM?............................86

23) Which infectious diseases are increased in type 2 DM?....................................86

24) How is serious intercurrent medical illness in type 2 DM managed?........................87

25) What are the criteria for testing for diabetes or prediabetes in asymptomatic adults?......88

26) What is the role of metformin in prediabetes?..89

27) What can be done for the primary prevention of stroke in patients with type 2 DM?........89

DIABETIC KETOACIDOSIS (DKA) (86) 90

Etiopathogenesis (14) 90

1) What are the 3 important features of DKA?..90

2) What are the two hormonal abnormalities responsible for the development of DKA?..........91

3) What causes increased Ketone production in DKA?...91

4) Which are the other hormones that contribute to the development of DKA? 91

5) What causes hyperglycemia in DKA?..92

6) What is the role of hepatic gluconeogenesis and glycogenolysis in the pathogenesis of DKA? 92

7) What is the role of lipolysis in the pathogenesis of DKA? 92

8) What causes dehydration in DKA?..92

9) How much is the free water loss in DKA?..93

10) What is the overall electrolyte loss in DKA? 94

11) What causes potassium loss in DKA?..94

12) What percent of patients with DKA presents with low serum potassium levels?...............95

13) What causes sodium loss in DKA? 95

14) What causes anion gap metabolic acidosis in DKA?...95

Clinical features (8) 96

1) When does DKA develop in type 2 diabetes?..96

2) What is the most common precipitating cause of DKA?......................................96

3) What are the most common early symptoms of DKA? 97

4) What are physical findings of diabetic ketoacidosis (DKA)?...............................98

5) What are signs of dehydration in DKA?..98

6) What are signs of acidosis in DKA?...98

7)	Why does Kussmaul breathing occur in DKA?	99
8)	Are mental changes typical in DKA?	99

Lab investigations (24) 99

1)	Which lab studies are performed in DKA?	99
2)	When should lab testing in DKA be repeated?	100
3)	What are the typical lab findings seen in DKA?	100
4)	What is the biochemical definition of DKA?	101
	Biochemical definition of DKA	101
5)	How are mild, moderate, and severe DKA defined?	101
6)	What conditions cause euglycemic DKA?	101
7)	Which is a true keto acid?	102
8)	Which is the predominant serum ketone body present in DKA?	102
9)	Is urine testing for ketones necessary to diagnose diabetic ketoacidosis (DKA)?	103
10)	What can cause a false-negative nitroprusside testing in DKA?	103
11)	Can a urine dipstick test for ketones be negative in DKA?	103
12)	What does Ketostix measure in DKA?	103
13)	What can cause a false-positive urine nitroprusside test?	104
14)	Are venous blood samples for biochemical studies sufficiently reliable in the management of DKA?	104
15)	How does serum potassium levels change in DKA?	104
16)	How does serum sodium levels change in DKA?	104
17)	How will you assess the degree of acidosis in DKA?	105
18)	What is the expected anion gap in DKA?	105
19)	What is the cause of the elevated anion gap in DKA?	105
20)	What is the role of plasma osmolarity in the evaluation of DKA?	105
21)	How will you evaluate treatment response?	105
22)	What is the role of ECG in the workup of DKA?	106
23)	What does elevated serum amylase and lipase in DKA mean?	106
24)	What are the diagnostic problems in DKA?	106

Management (40) 107

1)	What is the first step in the treatment of DKA?	107
2)	What is the first priority when treating patients with DKA?	107
3)	How will you manage a case of DKA?	108
4)	What is the schedule for restoring fluids during treatment of DKA?	108
5)	How will you replete ECF volume and free water deficits in DKA?	109
6)	When is isotonic saline changed to one-half isotonic saline?	109
7)	How will you correct potassium deficits in DKA?	110
8)	How does administration of insulin affect potassium level?	110

9) How will you initiate insulin therapy in DKA?..110
10) How will you give insulin in DKA? 111
11) What is the initial insulin dose for DKA?..111
12) What is the indication for delaying the initiation of insulin therapy in DKA?....................112
13) What are the advantages of rapid-acting insulin analogs over regular insulin in DKA? 112
14) What is the role for long- or intermediate-acting insulin in the management of DKA?.....112
    Acute management of DKA..112
    After recovery from ketoacidosis..112
15) How does insulin therapy lower the serum glucose concentration in DKA?......................113
16) How much can volume repletion alone reduce serum glucose initially? 113
17) What is the optimal rate of glucose decline in DKA?...114
18) Should insulin therapy begin before hypokalemia is treated in DKA?...............................114
19) When is potassium chloride administered in the treatment of DKA? 114
20) When should potassium replacement be initiated in DKA? 114
21) How often should serum potassium levels be monitored in the treatment of DKA?........115
22) How is acidosis treated in DKA? 115
23) When is sodium bicarbonate indicated in DKA?..115
24) What are the indications for phosphate replacement in DKA? 116
25) Which patients are primarily affected by cerebral edema during treatment of DKA?.......116
26) What are the diagnostic features of cerebral edema in DKA? 117
27) How is cerebral edema managed in DKA? 117
28) How is myocardial injury treated in DKA? 117
29) How do you monitor response to treatment of DKA?...118
30) Not used for monitoring resolution of DKA 118
31) Is monitoring with arterial blood gases necessary during the treatment of DKA?............119
32) What is the alternative to monitoring venous pH? 119
33) What is the role of anion gap in the management of DKA? 119
34) What is the alternative to monitoring anion gap?..119
35) Is monitoring capillary blood beta-hydroxybutyrate necessary during the treatment of DKA? 119
36) Why do almost all patients develop a normal anion gap acidosis during the resolution phase of the ketoacidosis?..119
37) Which are the two most common complications of the treatment of DKA? 120
38) How do you decide whether DKA has been resolved? 120
39) When can patients with DKA be discharged from the hospital? 120
40) How will you manage the transition from IV insulin to subcutaneous insulin?.................120

HYPEROSMOLAR HYPERGLYCEMIC STATE (HHS) (15) 121

1) What is HHS? 121
2) What is the underlying mechanism of HHS? 123
3) How does HHS present? 123
4) How does DKA and HHS differ clinically? 123
5) What are the diagnostic features of HHS? 124
6) How much is the free water loss in HHS? 124
7) Why is ketosis absent in HHS? 125
8) What causes the hyperosmolarity in HHS? 125
9) How does hyperglycemia affect serum sodium concentration? 125
10) What does an elevated serum Na concentration mean in HHS? 126
11) Which patients are most likely to develop hyperosmolar hyperglycemic state (HHS)? 126
12) What are the precipitating causes of HHS? 127
13) How do you decide whether HHS has resolved? 128
14) How will you manage the transition from IV insulin to subcutaneous insulin? 128
15) What is the mortality rate for HHS? 128

TYPE 2 DIABETES MELLITUS (190 Q&A)

Etiopathogenesis (15)

1) What are the top 3 countries in the number of people with diabetes?

Type 2 diabetes is by far the most common type of diabetes in adults (>90 percent). The top countries in the number of people with diabetes are currently India, China, the United States, Indonesia, Japan, Pakistan, Russia, Brazil, Italy, and Bangladesh.

2) What is the pathophysiology of type 2 DM?

Type 2 diabetes mellitus is characterized by hyperglycemia, insulin resistance, and relative impairment in insulin secretion. Its pathogenesis is only partially understood but both genetic and environmental factors, such as obesity, are important.

Pathogenesis of type 2 DM

---

1. Resistance to insulin action
2. Inadequate insulin secretion, and
3. Excessive or inappropriate glucagon secretion. **See figure below.**

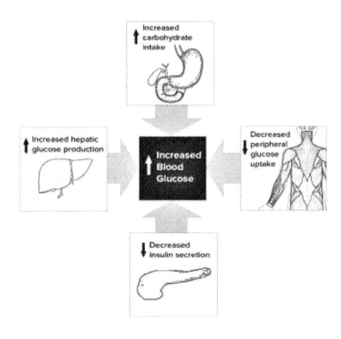

3) How does type 2 DM develop?

Type 2 diabetes mellitus is usually caused by a combination of insulin resistance (liver and muscle) and defective insulin secretion by pancreatic beta cells; these are due to a complex interaction among many genetic and environmental factors. The vast majority of patients have a genetic risk for type 2 diabetes.

Insulin resistance has been attributed to elevated levels of free fatty acids and proinflammatory cytokines in plasma. Insulin resistance leads to decreased glucose transport into muscle cells, elevated hepatic glucose production, and increased breakdown of fat.

The most important environmental risk factors in most patients who develop type 2 diabetes are increased weight gain and decreased physical activity. Insulin resistance may, at least in part, be related to substances secreted by adipocytes ("adipokines," including leptin, adiponectin, tumor necrosis factor-alpha, and resisting).

There is a role for excess glucagon. In type 2 diabetes, the reciprocal relationship between the glucagon-secreting alpha cell and the insulin-secreting beta cell is lost, leading to hyperglucagonemia and hence the consequent hyperglycemia.

4) What is the role of beta-cell dysfunction in the pathophysiology of type 2 DM?

Beta-cell dysfunction is a major factor across the spectrum of prediabetes to diabetes. Beta-cell dysfunction develops early in the pathologic process and does not necessarily follow the stage of insulin resistance.

Type 1 diabetes is characterized by autoimmune destruction of the pancreatic beta cells, leading to absolute insulin deficiency.

5) How does obesity affect the risk of developing type 2 diabetes mellitus (DM)?

90% of individuals with type 2 diabetes mellitus are overweight or have obesity.

6) What two factors must be present for type 2 DM to occur?
For type 2 diabetes mellitus to occur, both insulin resistance and inadequate insulin secretion must exist. All overweight individuals have insulin resistance, but diabetes develops only in those who cannot increase insulin secretion sufficiently to compensate for their insulin resistance. Their insulin concentrations may be high, yet inappropriately low for the level of glycemia.

7) How does insulin resistance affect glucose tolerance in type 2 DM?
In the progression from normal to abnormal glucose tolerance, postprandial blood glucose levels increase first. Eventually, fasting hyperglycemia develops as suppression of hepatic gluconeogenesis fails. Increased glucagon levels and increased glucose-dependent insulinotropic polypeptide (GIP) levels accompany glucose intolerance. However, the postprandial glucagon like peptide-1 (GLP-1) response is unaltered.

8) How does insulin resistance affect lipid accumulation and how is it managed?
Insulin resistance is associated with increased lipid accumulation in liver and smooth muscle, but not with increased myocardial lipid accumulation. Persistent lipid abnormalities remain in patients with diabetes despite the use of lipid-modifying drugs. Increasing the statin dose and the addition of other lipid-modifying agents are needed.

9) What are the etiologic factors of type 2 DM?
The etiology of type 2 diabetes mellitus involves complex interactions between environmental and genetic factors; the disease develops when a diabetogenic lifestyle (ie, excessive caloric intake, inadequate caloric expenditure, obesity) is superimposed on a susceptible genotype.

10) What are the major risk factors for type 2 diabetes mellitus (DM)?
The major risk factors for type 2 diabetes mellitus are the following:

1. Age greater than 45 years

2. *Family history of type 2 diabetes in a first-degree relative (eg,)*
   a. parent or sibling - two to three-fold increased risk of developing diabetes
   b. five- to sixfold in those with both a maternal and paternal history of type 2 diabetes.

3. Obesity or weight greater than desirable body weight
   a. Obesity induces resistance to insulin-mediated peripheral glucose uptake
   b. obesity is the most important modifiable risk factor for type 2 diabetes

4. Fat distribution
   a. Highest risk in those subjects with central or abdominal obesity, as measured by waist circumference or waist-to-hip circumference ratio

5. Prediabetes (see table below)

6. Hypertension (>140/90 mm Hg)

7. Dyslipidemia (HDL cholesterol level < 40 mg/dL or triglyceride level >150 mg/dL)

8. History of gestational diabetes mellitus or of delivering a baby with a birth weight of over 4kg

9. Polycystic ovarian syndrome (which results in insulin resistance)

*Prediabetes**

- FPG 100 to 125 mg/dL – IFG
- 2-hour post-load glucose on the 75 g OGTT 140 to 199 mg/dL – IGT
- HbA1C 5.7 to 6.4%

For all 3 tests, risk is continuous, becoming greater at higher ends of the range.

11) What is the rate of progression from IGT to overt diabetes?

The rate of progression from IGT to overt diabetes varies among different populations. The incidence rates of type 2 diabetes among patients with IGT ranges from 35 to 85 per 1000 person-years. Obesity (BMI, waist-to-hip ratio, and waist circumference) are positively associated with the incidence of type 2 diabetes.

Subjects who have only IGT generally do not develop the microvascular complications of diabetes such as retinopathy and nephropathy. They are, however, at substantially increased risk for developing macrovascular disease (coronary artery disease, stroke).

IFG (blood sugar of 100 to 125 mg/dL) increases the risk of developing type 2 diabetes. Fasting glucose levels less than 100 mg/mL are considered normal; however, subjects with fasting glucose values in the higher quintiles of normal range are at increased risk for developing type 2 diabetes.

Individuals with isolated IFG have hepatic insulin resistance; those with isolated IGT predominantly have muscle insulin resistance and normal or slightly reduced hepatic insulin sensitivity. Subjects with abnormalities in both tests have hepatic and muscle insulin resistance, which confers an increased risk of progressing to diabetes compared with having only one abnormality.

12) What genes are associated with an increased risk of type 2 DM?

The genetics of type 2 diabetes are complex and not completely understood. Identified genetic variants account for only about 10% of the heritable component of most type 2 diabetes. The one gene with the strongest effect on susceptibility is the transcription factor 7–like 2 (TCF7L2) gene.

13) What genes are associated with maturity onset diabetes of youth (MODY)?

The syndrome known as maturity onset diabetes of youth (MODY) accounts for 2-5% of individuals with type 2 diabetes; they present at a young age and have mild disease. The trait is autosomal dominant. To date, 11 MODY subtypes have been identified. Most of the MODY subtypes are associated with diabetes only; however, MODY type 5 is associated with renal cysts, and MODY type 8 is associated with exocrine pancreatic dysfunction.

14) What are the causes of secondary diabetes?

The most common causes of secondary diabetes are as follows:

- Diseases of the pancreas that destroy the pancreatic beta cells (eg, hemochromatosis, pancreatitis, cystic fibrosis, pancreatic cancer)

- Hormonal syndromes that interfere with insulin secretion (eg, pheochromocytoma)

- Hormonal syndromes that cause peripheral insulin resistance (eg, acromegaly, Cushing syndrome, pheochromocytoma)

- Drugs (eg, phenytoin, glucocorticoids, estrogens)

15) What causes metabolic syndrome (syndrome X)?

The metabolic syndrome (also called syndrome X) is due to insulin resistance. Metabolic syndrome due to insulin resistance can occur in patients with overtly normal glucose tolerance, prediabetes, or diabetes. Eventually, clinically apparent insulin resistance develops. An elevated fasting blood glucose or triglyceride level may be the first indication of insulin resistance.

Clinical features (5)

1) What symptoms suggest DM?

The majority of patients with type 2 diabetes are asymptomatic, and their disease remains undiagnosed for many years; hyperglycemia is noted on routine laboratory evaluation, prompting further testing.

Classic symptoms of hyperglycemia

- Polyuria
- Polydipsia
- Polyphagia
- Weight loss
- Nocturia, and
- Blurred vision

Other symptoms that may suggest hyperglycemia include lower extremity paresthesias, or yeast infections, particularly balanitis in men.

Polyuria occurs when the serum glucose concentration rises significantly above 180 mg/dL), exceeding the renal threshold for glucose reabsorption, which leads to increased urinary glucose excretion.

Glycosuria causes osmotic diuresis (ie, polyuria) and hypovolemia, which in turn can lead to polydipsia.

The diagnosis of diabetes mellitus is easily established when a patient presents with classic symptoms of hyperglycemia (increased thirst, polyuria, weight loss, blurry vision) and has a random plasma glucose value of 200 mg/dL or higher.

Rarely adults with type 2 diabetes can present with a hyperosmolar hyperglycemic state, characterized by marked hyperglycemia, severe dehydration, and obtundation, but without ketoacidosis.

Diabetic ketoacidosis (DKA) as the presenting symptom of type 2 diabetes is also uncommon in adults but may occur under certain circumstances (usually severe infection or other acute illness).

2) What are the symptoms of catabolism?
   1. Polyuria
   2. Polydipsia
   3. Unintentional weight loss.

3) How will you take a focused history in a patient with established type 2 DM?

In patients with known type 2 diabetes, inquire about the duration of the patient's diabetes. The duration of diabetes is significant because the chronic complications of diabetes are related to the length of time the patient has had the disease. Also find out about the care the patient is currently receiving for the disease.

A focused diabetes history should also include the following questions:

- Is the patient's diabetes generally well controlled (with near-normal blood glucose levels)? - Patients with poorly controlled blood glucose levels heal more slowly and are at increased risk for infection and other complications

- Does the patient have symptoms of hyperglycemia? E.g., recent polyuria, polydipsia, nocturia, or weight loss

- Does the patient have hypoglycemic reactions? If so, when, how often, and how does the patient treat these episodes? - If the patient has episodes of severe hypoglycemia, there is a risk of losing consciousness; this possibility must be addressed, especially if the patient drives or has significant underlying neuropathy or cardiovascular disease

- Does the patient have hypoglycemia unawareness (ie, does the patient lack the adrenergic warning signs of hypoglycemia)? - Hypoglycemia unawareness indicates an increased risk of subsequent episodes of hypoglycemia

- Does the patient have diabetic nephropathy that might alter the use of medications or IV radiographic contrast material?
- Does the patient have macrovascular disease, such as coronary artery disease that should be considered as a source of acute symptoms?

- When was the patient's hemoglobin A1c last measured, and what was it?

- What is the patient's immunization history? Eg, Covid, influenza, pneumococcal, hepatitis B, tetanus, herpes zoster.

As circumstances dictate, additional questions may be warranted, as follows:

- Retinopathy - When was the patient's last dilated eye examination, and what were the results?

- Nephropathy - Does the patient have known kidney disease; what were the dates and results of the last measurements of urine protein and serum creatinine levels?

- Does the patient have hypertension? What medications are taken?

- Does the patient have CAD?

- Peripheral vascular disease - Does the patient have claudication or a history of vascular bypass?

- Has the patient had a stroke or transient ischemic attack?

- What are the patient's most recent lipid levels; is the patient taking lipid-lowering medication?

- Does the patient have a history of neuropathy or are symptoms of peripheral neuropathy or autonomic neuropathy present (including impotence if the patient is male)?

- Does the patient have a history of foot ulcers or amputations; are any foot ulcers present?

- Are frequent infections a problem; at what site?

4) What findings should be noted during foot exams for type 2 diabetes mellitus (DM)?

The dorsalis pedis and posterior tibialis pulses should be palpated, and their presence or absence noted. This is particularly important in patients who have foot infections, because poor lower-extremity blood flow can slow healing and increase the risk of amputation.

Documenting lower-extremity sensory neuropathy is useful in patients who present with foot ulcers because decreased sensation limits the patient's ability to protect the feet and ankles. This can be assessed by reflexes, position, and/or vibration sensation.

5) What are the indications for diabetes screening in asymptomatic adults?

Criteria for Testing for Diabetes or Prediabetes in Asymptomatic Adults

1. Testing should be considered in adults with overweight or obesity (BMI ≥23 kg/m^2) who have one or more of the following risk factors:

   • *First-degree relative with diabetes*

   • *History of CVD*

   • *Hypertension (≥140/90 mmHg or on therapy for hypertension)*

   • *HDL cholesterol level <35 mg/dL (0.90 mmol/L) and/or a triglyceride level >250 mg/dL (2.82 mmol/L)*

   • *Women with polycystic ovary syndrome*

   • *Physical inactivity*

   • *Other clinical conditions associated with insulin resistance (e.g., severe obesity, acanthosis nigricans)*

2. Patients with prediabetes (A1C ≥5.7%), impaired glucose tolerance, or impaired fasting glucose) should be tested yearly.

3. Women who were diagnosed with GDM should have lifelong testing at least every 3 years.

4. For all other patients, testing should begin at age 45 years.

5. If results are normal, testing should be repeated at a minimum of 3-year intervals, with consideration of more frequent testing depending on initial results and risk status.

6. HIV

Diagnosis (24)

1) What are the ADA diagnostic criteria for type 2 DM?
Updated: Jul 13, 2021. Diagnostic criteria by the American Diabetes Association (ADA) include the following:

1. A fasting plasma glucose (FPG) level of 126 mg/dL or higher (fasting is defined as no caloric intake for at least 8 hours), OR

2. A 2-hour plasma glucose level of > 200 mg/dL during a 75-g oral glucose tolerance test (OGTT), OR

3. A random plasma glucose of >200 mg/dL in a patient with classic symptoms of hyperglycemia or hyperglycemic crisis, OR

4. An HbA1c level of 6.5% or higher.

If unequivocal hyperglycemia is absent, then HbA1c and FPG should be confirmed by repeat testing. However, if both FPG and A1C are concordant for the diagnosis of diabetes, additional testing is not needed. OGTT is not commonly used (except during pregnancy) owing to its inconvenience.

2) What is stress hyperglycemia?
Transient hyperglycemia may occur during severe illness in adults without known diabetes mellitus. This is a consequence of increased serum concentrations of cortisol, catecholamines, glucagon, and growth hormone, leading to increased gluconeogenesis, glycogenolysis and insulin resistance.

3) What conditions can interfere with FPG test results
Conditions that can interfere with FPG include:
- delayed or improper sample handling (samples should be collected in tubes that inhibit glycolysis and should not be left at room temperature prior to assay),
- inadequate duration of fasting,
- recent illness or physical activity,

- acute stress, and
- certain medications.

4) What conditions can interfere with HbA1c test results?
Conditions that can interfere with HbA1C include:
- Hemoglobinopathies,
- Conditions that alter hemoglobin or red blood cell lifespan.

5) How is prediabetes defined?

Prediabetes is defined by a fasting blood glucose level of 100-125 mg/dL or a 2-hour post-oral glucose tolerance test (post-OGTT) glucose level of 140-200 mg/dL (see table below). Prediabetes often precedes overt type 2 diabetes. Persons with prediabetes are at increased risk for macrovascular disease. If the diagnostic test is consistent with prediabetes, it should be repeated annually.

Criteria for the Screening and Diagnosis of Prediabetes and Diabetes

	Prediabetes	Diabetes
A1C	5.7–6.4%*	≥6.5%
Fasting plasma glucose	100–125 mg/dL*	≥126 mg/dL†
2-hour plasma glucose during 75-g OGTT	140–199 mg/dL*	≥200 mg/dL†
Random plasma glucose	—	≥200 mg/dL‡

*For all three tests, risk is continuous, extending below the lower limit of the range and becoming disproportionately greater at the higher end of the range.

†In the absence of unequivocal hyperglycemia, diagnosis requires two abnormal test results from the same sample or in two separate samples

‡Only diagnostic in patients with classic symptoms of hyperglycemia or hyperglycemic crisis.

6) What tests are needed to confirm a diagnosis of DM if unequivocal hyperglycemia is absent?

If unequivocal hyperglycemia is absent, then HbA1c, FPG, and OGTT results should be confirmed by repeat testing. The diagnosis of diabetes is confirmed if-
- both the A1C and fasting plasma glucose are above their diagnostic thresholds,
- if consecutive A1C levels are ≥6.5 percent,
- or if two consecutive fasting plasma glucose levels are ≥126 mg/dL.

7) What additional testing is required if 2 different test results are discordant for DM diagnosis?

If a patient has had 2 different tests and the results are discordant, the test that has a result above the diagnostic threshold should be repeated. A second abnormal result on this test will confirm the diagnosis.

8) What are the criteria for screening for type 2 diabetes or prediabetes in asymptomatic adults?

Criteria for testing for diabetes or prediabetes in asymptomatic adults

1. Testing should be considered in overweight or obese (BMI ≥23 kg/m² in Asians) adults who have one or more of the following risk factors:
    - First-degree relative with diabetes
    - History of CVD
    - Hypertension (≥140/90 mmHg or on therapy for hypertension)
    - HDL cholesterol level <35 mg/dL and/or a triglyceride level >250 mg/dL
    - Women with polycystic ovary syndrome
    - Physical inactivity
    - Other clinical conditions associated with insulin resistance (eg, severe obesity, acanthosis nigricans)
2. Patients with prediabetes (A1C ≥5.7%, IGT, or IFG) should be tested yearly.
3. Women who were diagnosed with GDM should have lifelong testing at least every 3 years.
4. For all other patients, testing should begin at age 45 years.
5. If results are normal, testing should be repeated at a minimum of 3-year intervals, with consideration of more frequent testing depending on initial results and risk status.

BMI: body mass index; CVD: cardiovascular disease; HDL: high-density lipoprotein; A1C: glycated hemoglobin; IGT: impaired glucose tolerance; IFG: impaired fasting glucose; GDM: gestational diabetes mellitus.

9) What testing should be performed in an asymptomatic patient with random serum glucose level that suggests DM (>140 mg/dL)?

In asymptomatic patients whose random serum glucose level suggests diabetes (>140 mg/dL), a FPG or HbA1c level should be measured. An FPG level of 100-125 mg/dL is considered an impaired fasting glucose (IFG), and an FPG level of less than 100 mg/dL is considered a normal fasting glucose. However, an FPG of 91-99 mg/dL is a strong independent predictor of future type 2 diabetes.

10) What HbA1c levels are considered diagnostic for prediabetes and diabetes mellitus (DM)?

< 5.7% = Normal
> 6.4% - Diagnostic for DM. HbA1c at 7% has a specificity of 100%.
5.7% to 6.4% - Diagnostic of prediabetes; increased risk of developing diabetes over the subsequent 5-8 years.

11) What HbA1c levels are predictive of myocardial infarction risk?

Each 1% increase independently predicts a 20% increase in odds of experiencing a myocardial infarction after accounting for other risk factors, including diabetes.

12) What timespan does glycated hemoglobin measurements reflect?

HbA1c measurements are the criterion standard for monitoring long-term glycemic control. Measurement of glycated hemoglobin reflects plasma glucose levels over the preceding 2-3 months. Binding of glucose to hemoglobin A occurs over the lifespan of a red blood cell (120 days).

13) How does a serum glucose measurement compare to a plasma glucose measurement in DM?

A serum glucose measurement (commonly obtained on chemistry panels) may be significantly lower than a plasma glucose measurement.

14) How are capillary whole blood measurements used in the diagnosis of DM?

Capillary whole blood measurements are not recommended for the diagnosis of diabetes mellitus, but they are valuable for assessment of patients in acute care situations.

15) What are the WHO diagnostic criteria for impaired glucose tolerance?
- FPG of less than 126 mg/dL, if measured, and
- Venous plasma glucose of 140 mg/dL to just below 200 mg/dL 2 hours after a 75-g glucose load with one intervening plasma glucose value at or above 200 mg/dL.

IGT is not a clinical entity but a risk factor for future diabetes and/or adverse outcomes. The risk of future diabetes, premature death, and cardiovascular disease begins to increase at 2-hour plasma glucose levels below the IGT range.

These criteria are a better predictor of increased macrovascular risk than IFG or prediabetes. Presumably, patients with IFG are at increased risk for development of diabetes mellitus, but their risk for macrovascular disease does not appear to be the same as for patients with IGT (which is about the same as for patients with frank type 2 diabetes mellitus).

16) How is type 2 DM different from type 1 DM?

Unlike patients with type 1 diabetes mellitus, patients with type 2 are not absolutely dependent on insulin for life. However, many patients with type 2 diabetes are ultimately treated with insulin. Because they retain the ability to secrete some endogenous insulin, they are considered to require insulin but not to depend on insulin.

Patients with type 2 diabetes are generally obese and may have acanthosis nigricans and/or hirsutism in conjunction with thick necks and chubby cheeks.

17) What are the clinical features that suggest type 1 diabetes?
There are certain clinical features that, if present at any age, suggest the diagnosis of type 1 diabetes. These include:
- marked and otherwise unexplained recent weight loss (irrespective of the initial weight),
- a short history with severe symptoms (polyuria, polydipsia), and
- the presence of moderate or greater ketonuria.

Diabetic ketoacidosis at first presentation suggests that the patient has type 1 diabetes and will require lifelong insulin treatment, although there are exceptions to this general rule.

A personal or family history of autoimmune disease (eg, hypo- or hyperthyroidism, celiac sprue) without family history of type 2 diabetes, especially in a patient without a history of overweight, is also suggestive of type 1 diabetes.

18) How will you differentiate type 2 from type 1 DM?
Patients with type 1 diabetes require insulin for survival. In contrast, treatment of type 2 diabetes consists of lifestyle measures and a variety of other medications, with insulin introduced if those prove inadequate. Therefore, it is important to correctly determine whether a patient has type 1 or type 2 diabetes.

Type 2 and type 1 disease can usually be differentiated by history, physical examination findings and simple laboratory tests. Patients with type 2 diabetes are generally obese and may have acanthosis nigricans and/or hirsutism in conjunction with thick necks and chubby cheeks.

A patient whose diabetes has been controlled with diet or an oral antidiabetic agent for longer than several months generally has type 2 diabetes. A lean patient who has had diabetes since childhood, who has always been dependent on insulin, or who has a history of diabetic ketoacidosis almost certainly has type 1 diabetes.

When the diagnosis of type 1 or type 2 diabetes is uncertain by clinical presentation, measure autoantibodies (eg, glutamic acid decarboxylase-65, islet cell, insulin, tyrosine phosphatase 2).

Clinical presentations that may warrant measurement of autoantibodies include:

- Catabolic presentation (eg, weight loss, ketonuria)

- Lean body habitus with no features of metabolic syndrome

- Personal history of autoimmune diseases

- Strong family history of autoimmune disease, including type 1 diabetes

- Overweight or obese adolescents or young adults.

Insulin levels generally are high early in the course of type 2 diabetes mellitus and gradually wane over time.

19) What is the role of C-peptide levels in differentiating type 1 and type 2 DM?

Measuring concentrations of insulin or C-peptide (marker for insulin secretion) rarely is necessary to differentiate type 2 diabetes from type 1 diabetes mellitus. A fasting C-peptide level of more than 1 ng/dL in a patient who has had diabetes for more than 1-2 years is suggestive of type 2 diabetes (ie, residual beta-cell function). Absence of a C-peptide response to carbohydrate ingestion may indicate total beta-cell failure.

20) What is "latent autoimmune diabetes in adults"?

Some individuals with adult-onset type 1 diabetes may be indistinguishable clinically from a patient with type 2 diabetes at presentation but will slowly progress to insulin dependence. This is referred to as "latent autoimmune diabetes in adults" (LADA).

LADA can be distinguished from type 2 diabetes by the presence of pancreatic autoantibodies, such as glutamic acid decarboxylase antibodies. These individuals may respond poorly to oral hypoglycemic drug therapy, and the use of sulfonylureas as initial therapy may cause earlier insulin dependence.

21) How is latent autoimmune diabetes of adults (LADA) differentiated from type 2 DM?

Latent autoimmune diabetes of adults (LADA) is a form of slow-onset type 1 diabetes that occurs in middle-aged (usually white) adults. It can be differentiated from type 2 diabetes by confirming the presence of antibodies against the GAD65 (65-kd isoform of glutamic acid decarboxylase), an enzyme found in pancreatic beta cells. Such patients may respond to insulin secretagogues for a brief period (months).

The best initial treatment strategy for LADA is unclear. Studies are required to determine whether early treatment with insulin or use of immunomodulator therapy may prevent disease progression.

22) Are autoantibodies useful in differentiating type 1 and type 2 DM?

Autoantibodies can be useful in differentiating between type 1 and type 2 diabetes. Islet-cell (IA2), anti-GAD65, and anti-insulin autoantibodies can be present in early type 1 diabetes, but not in type 2 disease. IA2 autoantibodies titers typically decrease after 6 months. Anti-GAD65 antibodies can be present at diagnosis of type 1 diabetes and are more likely to be persistently positive over time.

23) What testing is done in the ED for all patients with diabetes mellitus (DM)?

In the emergency department, a fingerstick glucose test is appropriate for virtually all patients with diabetes. All other laboratory studies should be individualized to the clinical situation.

24) How is metabolic syndrome (also called syndrome X) diagnosed?

It is diagnosed when a patient has at least 3 of the following 5 conditions:

1. Abdominal obesity

2. Elevated triglyceride level

3. Low level of HDL cholesterol

4. Elevated blood pressure

5. Fasting glucose value of 100 mg/dL or higher

Treatment (15)

1) What are the main goals of treatment for type 2 diabetes mellitus (DM)?
Goals of treatment are as follows:
1. Eliminate symptoms
2. Microvascular risk reduction (ie, eye and kidney disease)
   - Control of glycemia and blood pressure
3. Macrovascular risk reduction (ie, coronary, cerebrovascular, peripheral vascular)
   - Control of hypertension, lipids, and smoking cessation

- Improved glycemic management lowers the risk of microvascular complications in patients with type 2 diabetes.
- Vigorous cardiac risk reduction should be a top priority for all patients with type 2 diabetes.
   - Diet
   - Exercise
   - Smoking cessation
   - Blood pressure control
   - Reduction in serum lipids with a statin
   - Weight loss or maintenance
   - Aspirin for those with established atherosclerotic cardiovascular disease.

2) What are the guidelines for the initial management of type 2 DM?
Recommendations for the treatment of type 2 diabetes mellitus place the patient's condition, desires, abilities, and tolerances at the center of the decision-making process.

The 7 key points:
1. Diet, exercise, and education is the foundation of the treatment program
2. Individualize glycemic targets and glucose-lowering therapies
3. Use metformin as the optimal first-line drug unless contraindicated
4. After metformin, use 1 or 2 additional oral (eg, sulphonylurea) or injectable agents (eg, insulin, GLP-1 agonists)
5. Ultimately, insulin therapy alone or with other agents if needed to maintain blood glucose control
6. Where possible, all treatment decisions should involve the patient, with a focus on patient preferences, needs, and values
7. A major focus on cardiovascular risk reduction

3) What is medical nutrition therapy (MNT) for people with diabetes?
- In MNT, the dietary plan is tailored based on medical, lifestyle, and personal factors.
- For patients with type 2 diabetes and body mass index (BMI) ≥25 to 29.9 kg/m2 (overweight) or BMI ≥30 kg/m2 (obesity), major emphasis should be placed on weight reduction.
- For patients who are not trying to lose weight (not overweight), the goal of MNT is:
  - weight maintenance,
  - consistency in day-to-day carbohydrate intake, and
  - balanced nutritional content.

4) How effective is aggressive dietary modification in type 2 DM?
- Aggressive dietary modification is a highly effective method for weight loss.
  - Weight loss through dietary modification improves glycemic management and hypertension.
- A successful glycemic response to diet depends on the initial fasting blood glucose.
  - The degree of weight loss required to normalize the fasting blood glucose is:
    - 15% of initial body weight - if the initial FBS is 108 to 144 mg/dL

- 35% - if the initial value is 216 to 252 mg/dL.
- Despite the clear benefits of weight loss, only a small percentage of patients are able to attain and maintain substantial weight loss.

5) What is the role of weight loss in type 2 diabetes treatment?
   - Obesity management is first-line treatment.
   - Weight loss reduces blood glucose.
   - Weight loss reduces macrovascular complications.
     o Weight losses of 5-10% improve cardiovascular disease risk factors (ie, decreased HbA1c levels, reduced blood pressure, increase in HDL cholesterol, decreased plasma triglycerides).
     o Risk factor reduction is even greater with losses of 10-15% of body weight.

6) How should diet be managed in patients with type 2 DM?
   - Diet is one of the most important aspects of diabetes treatment.
     o The nutrition prescription for patients with type 2 diabetes should manage the "ABCs" of diabetes control:
       - Glycated hemoglobin (A1C),
       - Blood pressure, and
       - LDL cholesterol.
   - Caloric restriction is of first importance.
   - The best diet is one consisting of the foods that they are currently eating
     o Tailored for the individual patient.
   - Modest restriction of saturated fats and simple sugars is also reasonable.

7) What are the 5 components of medical nutrition therapy (MNT) in DM?
   - In MNT, the nutrition prescription is tailored for people with diabetes based on medical, lifestyle, and personal factors. The five components of MNT are:
     1. Weight management and increased physical activity,
     2. Caloric intake (balanced with caloric expenditure),

3. Day-to-day carbohydrate consistency (to avoid erratic blood glucose patterns and hypoglycemia),
   4. Nutritional content, and
   5. Meal timing (Meal content, quantity, and timing are particularly important for patients who are treated with insulin secretagogues or insulin regimens).

- Major emphasis should be placed on lowering caloric intake and inducing weight loss for patients with type 2 diabetes who are overweight (BMI ≥25 to 29.9 kg/m2) and obese (BMI ≥30 kg/m2).

8) What are the benefits of physical activity in type 2 DM?
   - Aerobic exercise alone or in combination with resistance training improves:
     - glycemic control,
     - circulating triglycerides,
     - systolic blood pressure, and
     - waist circumference.
   - Aerobic exercise improves glycemia markedly in some patients.
   - Exercise training of more than 150 minutes per week is associated with greater HbA1c reduction; however, physical activity helps lower HbA1c only when combined with dietary modifications.
   - Walking is accessible to most patients. A previously sedentary patient should start activities slowly.

9) When is cardiovascular evaluation needed prior to beginning a significant exercise regimen?
   1. Older patients
   2. Patients with previous evidence of atherosclerotic disease.
   3. Patients with long-standing disease
   4. Patients with multiple risk factors

10) How are glycemic management decisions made for type 2 DM?
Decisions about glycemic management are made on the basis of HbA1c measurements and the results of self-monitoring of blood glucose (SMBG).

11) What are the guidelines on the antidiabetic drug therapy in type 2DM?

The clinical guidelines on pharmacologic means of glycemic therapy in type 2 diabetes include the following:

- Employ a patient-centered approach to guide the choice of pharmacologic agents
    - Cardiovascular comorbid conditions
    - Hypoglycemia risk
    - Impact on weight
    - Cost
    - Risk for side effects
    - Patient preferences

- Metformin therapy is the preferred initial pharmacologic treatment for type 2 diabetes

- Consider early introduction of insulin if –
    - Weight loss
    - Symptoms of hyperglycemia are present
    - HbA1c >10%
    - Blood glucose levels are > 300 mg/dL

- Use a sodium-glucose cotransporter–2 (SGLT2) inhibitor or glucagon like peptide-1 receptor agonist (GLP-1 RA) in patients who have –
    - established atherosclerotic cardiovascular disease
    - indicators of high cardiovascular disease risk
    - established kidney disease
    - heart failure

- GLP-1 RAs, when possible, is preferred over insulin in patients who need greater glucose reduction than oral agents can provide

12) What are the drugs commonly used in the treatment of type 2 DM?

Agents used in diabetic therapy include the following:

1. Metformin (Biguanide)
2. Sulfonylureas
3. Meglitinide derivatives
4. Alpha-glucosidase inhibitors
5. Thiazolidinediones (TZDs)
6. Glucagon Like peptide–1 (GLP-1) agonists
7. Dipeptidyl peptidase IV (DPP-4) Inhibitors
8. Selective sodium-glucose transporter-2 (SGLT-2) inhibitors
9. Insulins
10. Amylinomimetic
11. Bile acid sequestrants
12. Dopamine agonists

Summary of glucose-lowering interventions

Intervention	A1C decrease (%)	Advantages	Disadvantages
Initial therapy			
Lifestyle change to decrease weight and increase activity	1.0 to 2.0	Broad benefits	Insufficient for most within first year owing to inadequate weight loss and weight regain
Metformin	1.0 to 2.0	Weight neutral	GI side effects, contraindicated with renal insufficiency (eGFR <30 mL/min/1.73 m^2)
Additional therapy			
Insulin (usually	1.5 to 3.5	No dose limit,	1 to 4 injections

with a single daily injection of intermediate- or long-acting insulin initially)		rapidly effective, improved lipid profile	daily, monitoring, weight gain, hypoglycemia, analogs are expensive
Sulfonylurea (shorter-acting agents preferred)	1.0 to 2.0	Rapidly effective	Weight gain, hypoglycemia (especially with glibenclamide)
GLP-1 receptor agonist (daily to weekly injections)	0.5 to 1.5	Weight loss, reduction in major adverse cardiovascular events (liraglutide, semaglutide, dulaglutide)	Requires injection, frequent GI side effects, expensive
Thiazolidinedione	0.5 to 1.4	Improved lipid profile (pioglitazone), potential decrease in MI (pioglitazone)	Fluid retention, HF, weight gain, bone fractures, potential increase in MI (rosiglitazone) and bladder cancer (pioglitazone)
Glinide	0.5 to 1.5	Rapidly effective	Weight gain, 3 times/day dosing, hypoglycemia
SGLT2 inhibitor	0.5 to 0.7	Weight loss, reduction in systolic blood pressure, reduced cardiovascular mortality in patients with	Vulvovaginal candidiasis, urinary tract infections, bone fractures, lower limb amputations, acute kidney injury, DKA,

		established CVD, improved renal outcomes in patients with nephropathy	long-term safety not established
DPP-4 inhibitor	0.5 to 0.8	Weight neutral	Possible increased risk of HF with saxagliptin, expensive
Alpha-glucosidase inhibitor	0.5 to 0.8	Weight neutral	Frequent GI side effects, 3 times/day dosing
Pramlintide	0.5 to 1.0	Weight loss	3 injections daily, frequent GI side effects, long-term safety not established, expensive

13) What is the initial treatment for asymptomatic patients with type 2 diabetes?
- Initial treatment of type 2 diabetes should begin with dietary modification, weight reduction, and exercise. These may achieve target glycated hemoglobin levels if compliance is optimal.
- Metformin therapy (in the absence of contraindications) may be initiated at the time of diabetes diagnosis.
    - Begin with 500 mg once daily with the evening meal
    - If tolerated, add a second 500 mg dose with breakfast.
    - Increase dose one tablet every one to two weeks as necessary to reach a total dose of 2000 mg per day.

14) What is the initial treatment for symptomatic patients with type 2 DM?
   - Patients who are symptomatic at initial presentation with diabetes (polyuria, polydipsia, or unintentional weight loss) may require transient treatment with insulin to reduce glucose toxicity (which may reduce beta-cell insulin secretion and worsen insulin resistance) or an insulin secretagogue to rapidly relieve symptoms such as polyuria and polydipsia.
   - For patients who do not want insulin, sulfonylurea is an alternative option
   - Insulin is always indicated for patients presenting with:
     - severe hyperglycemia (>300 mg/dL, A1C >9 percent with ketonuria)
     - spontaneous weight loss, or
     - in patients in whom it is difficult to distinguish type 1 from type 2 diabetes.

15) How will you manage patients with severe hyperglycemia without ketonuria or weight loss?
- Insulin or GLP-1 receptor agonists may be used (with or without metformin).
- For patients who are injection averse, initial therapy with high-dose sulfonylurea is an alternative option (glimepiride 4 or 8 mg once daily, immediate-release glipizide 10 mg twice daily, or gliclazide immediate-release 80 mg daily).
   - Contact the patient every few days to make dose adjustments
- Metformin can be started at the same time as the sulfonylurea, slowly titrating the dose upward.
   - Once the diet has been adequately modified and the metformin dose increased, the dose of sulfonylurea can be reduced and sometimes even discontinued.
- If adequate glycemic management is not achieved with metformin and high-dose sulfonylurea, start bedtime insulin or a GLP-1 receptor agonist.
   - When an injection is started, some clinicians continue sulfonylureas
   - Discontinue sulfonylureas if pre-prandial rapid-acting insulin is added.

- Metformin monotherapy is not helpful in improving symptoms in this setting, because the initial dose is low and increased over several weeks.

Metformin (12)

1) What are the benefits of metformin use in the treatment of type 2 DM?
   - Metformin improves hemoglobin A1c and lipid profile.
   - Metformin is the only oral diabetes drug that facilitates weight loss.
   - Metformin reduces macrovascular disease endpoints in obese patients.
   - Alone, they rarely cause hypoglycemia.
   - Relatively low cost
   - Good long-term safety profile

Metformin is used as monotherapy or in combination with sulfonylureas, thiazolidinediones, or insulin.

2) What are the beneficial actions of metformin in the treatment of type 2 DM?

Metformin lowers basal and postprandial plasma glucose levels by 5 mechanisms-
1. Decrease hepatic gluconeogenesis (primary effect)
2. Decrease intestinal absorption of glucose
3. Improve insulin sensitivity by increasing glucose utilization in muscle and liver, particularly after meals
4. Antilipolytic effect - lowers serum triglyceride and free fatty acid concentrations, thereby reducing substrate availability for gluconeogenesis
5. Decrease food intake and body weight.

As a result of the improvement in glycemic control, serum insulin concentrations decline slightly.

3) Why is metformin the preferred initial therapy?
   - Metformin is the preferred initial therapy because of:
     - glycemic efficacy,

- o absence of weight gain and hypoglycemia,
- o favorable cost, and
- o no adverse cardiovascular effects.
- Metformin is far less expensive and has more clinical practice experience than glucagon-like peptide 1 (GLP-1) receptor agonists and sodium-glucose co-transporter 2 (SGLT2) inhibitors.

4) What are the most common side effects of metformin?

The most common side effects of metformin are gastrointestinal, including a metallic taste in the mouth, mild anorexia, abdominal discomfort, and soft bowel movements or diarrhea. These symptoms are usually mild, transient, and minimized by taking the medication with food.

If gastrointestinal symptoms develop while taking metformin, institute a metformin holiday, which may lead to resolution of symptoms. After a period of non-use, metformin may be successfully resumed at the same or a lower dose with a slow titration of the immediate-release or extended-release formulation.

The incidence of lactic acidosis in metformin users is very low. Despite its rarity, lactic acidosis related to metformin is a concern because of the high case-fatality rate.

5) How do you titrate the dose of metformin?

The dose of metformin is titrated over 1-2 months. Begin with 500 mg once daily with the evening meal to minimize adverse GI effects; if tolerated, add a second 500 mg dose with breakfast. The dose can be increased slowly (one tablet every one to two weeks) until reaching the usual effective dose (1500 to 2000 mg/day).

6) What is the effect of metformin on vitamin B12 metabolism?

Metformin reduces intestinal absorption of vitamin B12 in up to 30 percent of patients and lowers serum vitamin B12 concentrations in 5 to 10 percent, but it only rarely causes megaloblastic anemia. In some patients, vitamin B12 deficiency may present as peripheral neuropathy.

7) Can you use metformin if the serum creatinine level is 1.5 mg/dL?

Metformin is not metabolized and is rapidly eliminated by the kidneys. Drug levels increase markedly in renal insufficiency. Metformin is contraindicated in patients with impaired renal function, as indicated by a serum creatinine level of greater than 1.5 mg/dL in men or of more than 1.4 mg/dL in women, or an estimated GFR of less than 45 mL/min. Lactic acidosis is an extremely rare, but serious, complication that may occur with drug accumulation.

Metformin also should not be used within 48 hours of IV iodinated contrast medium.

For patients taking metformin, measure A1C every three to six months; serum creatinine annually; and vitamin B12 annually, particularly in patients at risk for vitamin B12 deficiency due to decreased intake (eg, vegan diet) or absorption (eg, bariatric surgery).

8) What are the contraindications for metformin?

Metformin is contraindicated in patients with factors predisposing to lactic acidosis. These predisposing factors/contraindications are:

- Impaired kidney function (estimated glomerular filtration rate <30 mL/min/1.73 m2)

- Concurrent active or progressive severe liver disease

- Active alcohol abuse

- Unstable or acute heart failure at risk of hypoperfusion

- Past history of lactic acidosis during metformin therapy

- Decreased tissue perfusion or hemodynamic instability due to infection or other causes

The exact degree of kidney, cardiac, and liver function required for the safe use of metformin is uncertain. Stable compensated heart failure is not a contraindication to metformin use.

9) What are the recommendations for the addition of other oral drugs to metformin glycemic control?

Use metformin as first-line treatment for type 2 diabetes. After a successful initial response to metformin, the majority of patients have recurrence of hyperglycemia and require the addition of a second oral or an injectable agent. When a second oral therapy is needed, consider the addition of one of the following classes—sulfonylureas, thiazolidinediones, dipeptidyl peptidase IV (DPP-4) inhibitors, or selective sodium-glucose transporter–2 (SGLT-2) inhibitors—to metformin.

10) What is the indication for dual-drug therapy in the treatment of type 2 DM?

If the patient fails to safely achieve or sustain glycemic goals within 2-3 months, another medication should be added. The choice should be guided by patient characteristics (eg, a DPP-4 inhibitor if both postprandial and fasting glucose levels are elevated; a GLP-1 agonist if postprandial glucose levels are strongly elevated; a TZD if the patient has metabolic syndrome and/or nonalcoholic fatty liver disease).

Failure of initial therapy usually should result in addition of another class of drug rather than substitution. Reserve the use of substitution for cases in which patients experience intolerance to a drug because of adverse effects.

11) If 2 drugs are unsuccessful, what options for triple-drug therapy are available for type 2 DM?

If 2 drugs prove unsuccessful after 2-3 months, the next step is triple therapy. The third drug may be an oral agent from a third class of antidiabetic drugs, basal insulin (typically at bedtime), or the injectable drug exenatide. If basal insulin is used, the insulin dose is titrated to the fasting glucose concentration, which the patient can measure at home. Exenatide needs only 2 possible doses and although expensive, it avoids hypoglycemia.

The expense and adverse effect profile of TZDs make their use in an oral triple therapy approach less desirable.

12) A patient has persistent hyperglycemia even after metformin 2g daily and lifestyle intervention. What is the next drug to be added?
The therapeutic options for patients who have persistent hyperglycemia with lifestyle intervention and metformin are to add a second oral or injectable agent or to switch to insulin. There is no consensus on which option is most effective. Insulin is preferred in insulin-deficient, catabolic diabetes (eg, polyuria, polydipsia, weight loss). A GLP-1 receptor agonist may be used if the patient is not catabolic.

Sulfonylureas (6)

1) Which oral agent has the greatest efficacy for glycemic lowering?
Sulfonylureas (eg, glyburide, glipizide, glimepiride) have the greatest efficacy for glycemic lowering of any of the oral agents. However, that effect is only short-term and quickly dissipates.

2) What is the mechanism of action of sulfonylureas?
- Sulfonylureas are insulin secretagogues that stimulate insulin release from pancreatic beta cells.
- Sulfonylurea inhibits ATP-sensitive potassium channel (K-ATP channel) in the pancreatic beta cells leading to stimulation of insulin secretion. There is increased responsiveness of beta cells to glucose and amino acids, resulting in more insulin being released at all blood glucose concentrations.
- Sulfonylureas may also enhance peripheral sensitivity to insulin, but the clinical importance of this effect is minimal.

3) By what percentage does sulfonylureas reduce HbA1c?
- Sulfonylureas reduce HbA1c by 1-2% and blood glucose concentrations by about 20%.

4) Which are the sulfonylureas with a shorter duration of action?
- Glipizide, gliclazide and glimepiride have a relatively shorter duration with lower risk for hypoglycemia.

- First-generation sulfonylureas (eg, chlorpropamide, tolbutamide) are not commonly used owing to their long duration of action and increased risk for hypoglycemia.

5) How should sulfonylureas be used in the treatment of type 2 DM?
- Sulfonylureas can be used in patients who fail initial therapy with lifestyle intervention and metformin.
- A short-acting sulfonylurea (eg, glipizide, gliclazide and glimepiride) is an option for patients without established cardiovascular disease who have contraindications to or intolerance to metformin, particularly if cost is a concern.
- Sulfonylureas are generally not used in combination with insulin.
- The second-generation sulfonylureas (glipizide, glyburide, and glimepiride) can be given as once-daily regimens.

6) What is the most common side effect of sulfonylureas?
- Hypoglycemia is the most common side effect. Hypoglycemia is less common with shorter- (gliclazide, glipizide) than longer-acting (glyburide) sulfonylureas.
- Modest weight gain is a common side effect of sulfonylureas.

GLP-1 agonists (12)

1) What are the beneficial actions of glucagon-like peptide-1 (GLP-1) agonists in type 2 DM?

Injectable GLP-1 agonists (i.e., exenatide, liraglutide, albiglutide, dulaglutide) mimic the actions of the endogenous hormone incretin. Incretin hormones are synthesised by small intestinal L cells and are involved in the physiologic regulation of glucose homeostasis. Their actions are given below.

GLP-1 agonists actions

1. Stimulate glucose-dependent insulin release (as opposed to oral insulin secretagogues, which cause non–glucose-dependent insulin release and hypoglycemia)
2. Suppresses inappropriately elevated glucagon secretion

3. Slow gastric emptying
4. Weight loss (approximately 2 to 3 kg)
5. May prevent beta-cell apoptosis and may in time restore beta-cell mass.

In healthy individuals, ingestion of food results in release of gastrointestinal peptides (GLP-1 and GIP) as well as pancreatic beta cell hormones (insulin and amylin). GLP-1 and amylin, in particular, have inhibitory effects on gastric emptying, glucagon release, and appetite. Following the absorption of food, GLP-1 and GIP promote insulin secretion, otherwise known as the incretin effect. In diabetes, these steps are disrupted.

2) What are the indications for using GLP-1 receptor agonists?

GLP-1 receptor agonists are not considered as initial therapy for the majority of patients with type 2 diabetes. Initial therapy in most patients with type 2 diabetes should begin with diet, weight reduction, exercise, and metformin.

GLP-1 receptor agonists can be prescribed in combination with metformin (and/or another oral agent) for patients with persistent hyperglycemia on initial therapy with one or two oral agents and in whom weight loss or avoidance of hypoglycemia is a primary consideration.

The GLP-1 receptor agonists are effective in reducing cardiovascular disease (CVD) in patients with existing atherosclerotic CVD. When a decision has been made to use a GLP-1 receptor agonist in a patient with existing clinical atherosclerotic CVD, liraglutide, semaglutide, or dulaglutide is suggested based on the respective cardiovascular outcomes study results.

For patients without clinical ASCVD, use long- rather than short-acting GLP-1 receptor agonists. This is predominantly due to patient convenience.

3) What is the glycemic efficacy of GLP-1 receptor agonists?

GLP-1 receptor agonists reduce glycated hemoglobin by 0.55 to 1.4%. Longer-acting GLP-1 receptor agonists reduce A1C more than shorter-acting ones.

4) Which are the injectable GLP-1 agonists?

When a decision has been made to use a GLP-1 receptor agonist, exenatide (two daily injections or one weekly injection), lixisenatide (once-daily injection), liraglutide (once-daily injection), dulaglutide (once-weekly injection), or semaglutide (once-weekly injection or once-daily oral tablet) are available options.

5) Which are the long-acting GLP-1 receptor agonists that can be given once weekly injections?

Extended-release exenatide, dulaglutide, and semaglutide are long-acting GLP-1 receptor agonists given as a once-weekly injection.

6) Which glucagon like peptide-1 (GLP-1) agonist can be given orally in type 2 DM?
- Semaglutide is available in an oral form.
- Semaglutide may be administered as a once daily oral tablet or a weekly SC injection.
- The SC product is also indicated for cardiovascular risk reduction in adults with type 2 diabetes mellitus and heart disease.

7) How is exenatide given in type 2 DM?

The injectable suspension of exenatide is administered 2 mg SC once *weekly*. It is indicated when metformin and/or a sulfonylurea have not achieved glycemic control (not considered a first-line therapy). Nausea and injection site reactions occur in 10 percent of patients. Short-acting exenatide injectable solution is also available.

Albiglutide and dulaglutide are once-weekly SC injectable GLP-1 receptor agonists. They are indicated as an adjunct to diet and exercise to improve glycemic control in adults with type 2 diabetes mellitus.

8) What are the benefits of adding exenatide to insulin glargine in type 2 DM?

The addition of a GLP-1 agonist (eg, exenatide) to basal insulin (eg, glargine) achieves glycemic targets at reduced insulin dose and without insulin-induced weight gain. This benefit, however, is accompanied by a significant increase in adverse events such as nausea, diarrhea, vomiting, and headache. Once-weekly exenatide injections provides greater improvement in HbA1c and FPG levels than twice-daily preparation.

9) What are the benefits of combination therapy with GLP-1 receptor agonists and DPP-4 inhibitors?

Combination therapy with GLP-1 receptor agonists and dipeptidyl peptidase 4 inhibitors does not provide additive glucose-lowering effects, and thus, the combination should be avoided.

10) What is the role of liraglutide in the treatment of type 2 DM?
- Liraglutide is a *once-daily* SC injectable GLP-1 receptor agonist. It stimulates G-protein in pancreatic beta cells. It increases intracellular cyclic adenosine monophosphate (cAMP), leading to insulin release in the presence of elevated glucose concentrations.
- Liraglutide is not recommended as first-line pharmacologic therapy, because of potential serious adverse effects.
- Liraglutide may be used as monotherapy in addition to diet and exercise.
- Liraglutide may be used in combination with oral agents and basal insulin in adults with type 2 diabetes.
- Liraglutide is approved for risk reduction of major cardiovascular events (cardiovascular death, nonfatal myocardial infarction, and nonfatal stroke) in adults with type 2 diabetes mellitus and established cardiovascular disease.
- It is also indicated for children aged 10 years or older with type 2 diabetes mellitus.

11) What are the side effects of GLP-1 receptor agonists?
- The long-term safety of GLP-1 receptor agonists has not been established.
- The side effects of GLP-1 receptor agonists are predominantly gastrointestinal, particularly nausea, vomiting, and diarrhea.
- Injection site reactions (abscess, cellulitis, and necrosis)
- The risk of hypoglycemia is small. For the majority of patients in whom the addition of GLP-1 receptor agonists is prompted by poor glycemic control, a reduction in the dose of basal insulin, sulfonylureas, and glinides is not typically necessary.
- Angioedema and anaphylaxis – Rare.

12) What precautions should be taken before giving GLP-1 receptor agonists?
- Should not be used in patients with a history of pancreatitis.
- Not approved for use in those with type 1 diabetes.
- Should not be used in patients with a personal or family history of medullary thyroid cancer or multiple endocrine neoplasia 2A or 2B.
- Should be used with caution in patients with renal impairment.
- Must be used with caution in those with gastroparesis.

Dipeptidyl peptidase 4 (DPP-4) inhibitors (3)

1) Which are the DPP-4 inhibitors available for the treatment of type 2 diabetes?

Sitagliptin, saxagliptin, linagliptin, alogliptin, and vildagliptin are the DPP-4 inhibitors available for the treatment of type 2 diabetes.

2) What is the role of dipeptidyl peptidase IV inhibitors (DPP-4 inhibitors) in the treatment of type 2 DM?
- DPP-4 degrades the incretins GLP-1 and glucose-dependent insulinotropic peptide (GIP). DPP-4 inhibitors (eg, sitagliptin, saxagliptin, linagliptin) prolong the action of incretin hormones.
- The exact role for DPP-4 inhibitors for management of type 2 diabetes is unclear. They are not considered as initial therapy for the majority of patients with type 2 diabetes.

- DPP-4 inhibitors can be used as a monotherapy in patients who are intolerant of or have contraindications to metformin (eg, patients with chronic kidney disease), or other glucose-lowering agents.
- DPP-4 inhibitors can be considered as add-on drug therapy for patients who are inadequately controlled on metformin, a thiazolidinedione, SGLT2 inhibitor, or a sulfonylurea.
- They are given once daily and are weight neutral.

3) What are the benefits of linagliptin in the treatment of type 2 DM?
- Linagliptin is primarily eliminated via the enterohepatic system and is not a significant substrate for cytochrome-450 isoenzymes. Therefore, this drug has a low risk of drug-drug interaction and is safe to use in patients with renal insufficiency.
- Sitagliptin, saxagliptin, alogliptin, and vildagliptin require dose adjustment in patients with chronic kidney disease; they may be used in chronic kidney disease with proper dose adjustment.

SGLT-2 inhibitors (11)

1) How do sodium-glucose transporter-2 inhibitors act?
   - Sodium-glucose co-transporter 2 (SGLT2) inhibitors reduce blood glucose by increasing urinary glucose excretion.
   - SGLT2 is expressed in the proximal tubule and mediates reabsorption of 90 percent of the filtered glucose from the tubular lumen. SGLT-2 inhibitors (canagliflozin, dapagliflozin, empagliflozin, ertugliflozin) lower the renal glucose threshold (ie, the plasma glucose concentration that exceeds the maximum glucose reabsorption capacity of the kidney) in the proximal renal tubules. Lowering the renal glucose threshold results in reduced glucose reabsorption, increased urinary glucose excretion and decreased blood glucose.
   - SGLT2 inhibitors do not usually cause hypoglycemia.
   - SGLT2 inhibitors modestly decrease blood pressure and weight.

2) What is the glycemic efficacy of SGLT2 inhibitors?
SGLT2 inhibitors are relatively weak glucose-lowering agents, with mean reductions in A1C ranging between 0.5 to 1.0 percent

3) What is the role of SGLT2 inhibitors in the treatment of type 2 DM?
- SGLT2 inhibitors (canagliflozin, dapagliflozin, empagliflozin, ertugliflozin) are not considered as initial therapy for the majority of patients with type 2 diabetes.
- SGLT2 inhibitors are associated with only modest improvement in glycemia, are costly, and long-term safety data on the effects of prolonged glucosuria are lacking.
- In patients with cardiorenal comorbidities, many SGLT2 inhibitors have demonstrated benefit for cardiorenal outcomes.

SGLT2 inhibitors play a role in the following settings:
1. In patients with overt atherosclerotic cardiovascular disease not reaching glycemic goals with metformin and lifestyle modifications
    a. Empagliflozin, canagliflozin, and dapagliflozin, but not ertugliflozin

2. In patients with heart failure not reaching glycemic goals with metformin and lifestyle modifications
    a. Empagliflozin, canagliflozin, dapagliflozin, and ertugliflozin

3. In patients with urine albumin-to-creatinine ratio >300 mg/g and estimated glomerular filtration rate [eGFR] <90 mL/min/1.73 m2
    a. Canagliflozin, dapagliflozin

4. As a third-line agent in patients with inadequate glycemic control on two oral agents (eg, metformin and sulfonylurea) if for some reason combination metformin and insulin is not a therapeutic option

5. As a third-line agent in patients not adequately controlled on metformin and insulin therapy, in whom GLP-1 receptor agonists are contraindicated and increasing insulin dosing would lead to weight gain

6. As a second agent in patients with inadequate control on metformin who are unwilling or unable to consider injection

therapy and in whom weight gain and risk of hypoglycemia are a significant issue

4) What is the role of canagliflozin in the treatment of type 2 DM?
- Canagliflozin added to metformin and/or sulfonylureas reduces fasting glucose and HbA1C level.
- Canagliflozin added to insulin and to dipeptidyl peptidase-IV inhibitors also improves postprandial glucose levels and HbA1C levels.
- In adults with type 2 diabetes and diabetic nephropathy with albuminuria of more than 300 mg/day, canagliflozin is indicated to lower the chances of end-stage renal disease, cardiovascular death, and hospitalization for heart failure.

5) What are the indications for dapagliflozin in the treatment of type 2 DM?
- Dapagliflozin is indicated as an adjunct to diet and exercise to improve glycemic control in adults with type 2 diabetes mellitus. It can be employed as monotherapy, as initial therapy with metformin, or as an add-on to other oral glucose-lowering agents, including metformin, pioglitazone, glimepiride, sitagliptin, and insulin.
- Dapagliflozin should not be used if eGFR is < 60 mL/min/1.73 m2.
- Dapagliflozin is also indicated to lower the risk of being hospitalized for heart failure in diabetics with established cardiovascular disease or multiple cardiovascular risk factors.

6) What are the indications for empagliflozin in the treatment of type 2 DM?
- Empagliflozin is specifically indicated for the prevention of cardiovascular disease–related death in adults with type 2 diabetes who also have cardiovascular disease.
- Like dapagliflozin, empagliflozin is also approved as an adjunct to diet and exercise to improve glycemic control.

7) Which SGLT2 inhibitor is preferred in a patient with type 2 diabetes and a prior history of atherosclerotic cardiovascular disease?

Empagliflozin.

8) Which SGLT2 inhibitor is preferred in a patient with type 2 diabetes and heart failure or kidney disease?

In patients with type 2 diabetes and heart failure, all SGLT2 inhibitors have shown beneficial effects

9) What are the adverse effects of SGLT2 inhibitors?

The most common side effects of SGLT2 inhibitors are vulvovaginal candida infections and hypotension. Acute kidney injury, urinary tract infections, necrotizing fasciitis of the perineum, euglycemic diabetic ketoacidosis, increased risk of lower extremity amputation, and bone fractures have also been reported.

- Genitourinary tract infection - Two- to fourfold increased incidence of vulvovaginal candidiasis in 10 to 15 percent of women.
- Hypotension — SGLT2 inhibitors cause an osmotic diuresis and intravascular volume contraction. In older patients or in patients taking diuretics, ACE inhibitors, or angiotensin receptor blockers, SGLT2 inhibitors may cause symptomatic hypotension.
- Acute renal injury - Since the SGLT2 inhibitors can cause a mild degree of dehydration, they should be used with caution in conjunction with other medications that predispose to acute renal injury (NSAIDs, ACE inhibitors/ ARBs, diuretics) and comorbidities that might predispose to acute renal injury (hypovolemia, heart failure, liver injury).
- Bone fracture - In some studies, the incidence of fractures was higher in patients taking canagliflozin.
- Diabetic ketoacidosis — SGLT2 inhibitors increase the risk of DKA. The absence of substantial hyperglycemia delays recognition of the problem by both the patients and the clinicians. Serum ketones should be obtained in any patient with nausea, vomiting, or malaise while taking SGLT2 inhibitors, and SGLT2 inhibitors should be discontinued if acidosis is confirmed.

- Amputations —SGLT2 inhibitors, particularly canagliflozin, are associated with an increased risk of amputation.

10) What are the contraindications for SGLT2 inhibitors?

SGLT2 inhibitors should not be used for the treatment of hyperglycemia in patients with:
1. Type 1 diabetes
2. Type 2 diabetes and estimated glomerular filtration rate (eGFR) <30 mL/min/1.73 m2. SGLT2 inhibitors have renal benefits in patients with eGFR ≥30 mL/min/1.73m2.
3. Prior diabetic ketoacidosis

Avoid use of SGLT2 inhibitors in patients with the following conditions:
- Frequent bacterial urinary tract infections or genitourinary yeast infections.
- Low bone mineral density and high risk for fracture and falls.
- Foot ulceration (eg, neuropathy, foot deformity, vascular disease, and/or history of previous foot ulceration).
- Factors predisposing to DKA (eg, ketosis-prone type 2 diabetes, pancreatic insufficiency, drug, or alcohol addiction)
- Since the SGLT2 inhibitors can cause a mild degree of dehydration, they should be used with caution in conjunction with other medications that predispose to acute renal injury (NSAIDs, ACE inhibitors/ ARBs, diuretics) and comorbidities that might predispose to acute renal injury (hypovolemia, heart failure, liver injury).

11) How should a patient be evaluated prior to starting an SGLT2 inhibitor?
- Prior to starting an SGLT2 inhibitor, volume status and renal function (serum creatinine with eGFR) should be assessed. Hypovolemia should be corrected prior to initiating an SGLT2 inhibitor.
- Liver function should be assessed prior to initiation of canagliflozin or dapagliflozin.

- Patients at risk for falls and fractures may benefit from assessment of bone density.
- Patients using insulin or insulin secretagogues (sulfonylureas, glinides) may require a dose reduction with initiation of SGLT2 inhibitors to reduce the risk of hypoglycemia.

Meglitinides (4)

1) What are meglitinides?
Meglitinides (eg, repaglinide, nateglinide) are much shorter-acting insulin secretagogues than the sulfonylureas.

2) What is the mechanism of action of meglitinides?
- Repaglinide and nateglinide act similarly to sulfonylureas by regulating K-ATP channels in pancreatic beta cells, thereby increasing insulin secretion.
- Repaglinide has slightly superior glycemic efficacy compared with nateglinide.

3) How should meglitinides be used to treat type 2 diabetes mellitus (DM)?
- Meglitinides are most useful in patients who do not reach glycemic goals with metformin, particularly if there are contraindications to sulfonylureas.
- Meglitinides may be used in patients who have an allergy to sulfonylurea medications.
- Meglitinide monotherapy has efficacy similar to that of sulfonylureas but is considerably more expensive than sulfonylureas.
- Meglitinides have a similar risk for inducing weight gain as sulfonylureas do but carry less risk for hypoglycemia.
- For patients who have a highly variable diet or substantial postprandial hyperglycemia with large meals, repaglinide may be taken at those meals only.

4) Can repaglinide be used in patients with chronic kidney disease?
- Yes. Repaglinide is principally metabolized by the liver, with less than 10 percent renally excreted. Thus, it can be used safely in patients with chronic kidney disease.
- Nateglinide is hepatically metabolized, with renal excretion of active metabolites. It should be used with caution, if at all, in patients with chronic liver or advanced renal disease.

Alpha-glucosidase inhibitors (1)

1) What is the role of alpha-glucosidase inhibitors in the treatment of type 2 DM?

Alpha-glucosidase inhibitors (Acarbose, Miglitol) prolong the absorption of carbohydrates and thus help to prevent postprandial glucose surges. Their effect on glycemic control is modest, affecting primarily postprandial glycemic excursions. Their induction of flatulence greatly limits their use. They should be titrated slowly to reduce gastrointestinal intolerance.

Acarbose is absorbed to a small degree, so liver function abnormalities can occur rarely. Miglitol is not absorbed, so liver function abnormalities do not occur.

Thiazolidinediones (6)

1) What is the mechanism of action of thiazolidinediones?
- The only thiazolidinedione still used to any degree is pioglitazone. Pioglitazone acts as an insulin sensitizer; it improves the response of muscle and fat to insulin without increasing insulin secretion from the pancreas. Thus, pioglitazone increases glucose utilization by adipose tissue and muscle.
    - Pioglitazone activates peroxisome proliferator–activated receptor (PPAR) gamma with some PPAR-alpha agonist activity; this is a nuclear transcription factor that is important in fat cell differentiation and fatty acid metabolism.

- These drugs may have beta-cell preservation properties. They are the only antidiabetic agents that have been shown to slow the progression of diabetes (particularly in early disease).
- To a lesser degree, they decrease glucose production by the liver.

2) How should TZDs be used in the treatment of type 2 DM?
- Pioglitazone is not considered first-choice agent for patients with type 2 diabetes, due to adverse effects including increased risk of weight gain, fluid retention, heart failure, fractures, and the potential small increased risk of bladder cancer.
- Pioglitazone is used as monotherapy or in combination with sulfonylurea, metformin, meglitinide, DPP-4 inhibitors, GLP-1 receptor agonists, or insulin.
- Pioglitazone must be taken for 12-16 weeks to achieve maximal effect.

3) How effective are thiazolidinediones in the treatment of type 2 DM?

When used as monotherapy, thiazolidinediones reduce glycated hemoglobin values by 0.5 to 1.4 percentage points (efficacy between that of alpha-glucosidase inhibitors and sulfonylureas).

4) What are the adverse effects of thiazolidinediones to treat type 2 DM?
- Fluid retention (Edema)
    - Fluid retention is more prominent with concomitant insulin therapy.
    - Result from PPAR-gamma stimulation of sodium reabsorption by sodium channels in the luminal membrane of the collecting tubule cells.

- Heart failure
    - Fluid retention may induce or worsen heart failure in patients with left ventricular compromise and occasionally in patients with normal left ventricular function.

- Weight gain
    - Dose- and time-dependent.
    - Especially when TZDs are administered with insulin or insulin secretagogues.
- Bladder cancer
    - The use of pioglitazone for more than 2 years is weakly associated with an Increased bladder cancer risk; constant surveillance is needed.
    - Association is controversial
- Skeletal fractures
    - Thiazolidinediones decrease bone density and increase fracture risk, particularly in women.
- Macular edema
    - Diabetic macular edema can occur at least sporadically, but this is rare.

5) What are the contraindications for thiazolidinedione use?

Thiazolidinediones should not be used in patients with:
- Heart failure or any evidence of fluid overload
- History of fracture or at high risk for fracture (eg, postmenopausal women with low bone mass)
- Active liver disease (liver transaminases >2.5 times above the upper reference limit)
- Active or history of bladder cancer
- Type 1 diabetes
- Pregnancy
- Thiazolidinediones should be discontinued in patients who develop macular edema.

6) Can thiazolidinediones be used for diabetes prevention?

Using thiazolidinediones for diabetes prevention is not recommended. Thiazolidinediones are limited by adverse effects. Thus, the risks may outweigh the benefits.

Insulins (23)

1) Which are the commonly used insulin preparations?
   In type 2 diabetes, insulin is generally provided in three ways:
   1. As a basal supplement to suppress hepatic glucose production and maintain glucose levels at target in the fasting state -
        a. Intermediate-acting to long-acting preparation
             i. Neutral protamine Hagedorn [NPH]
             ii. Glargine
             iii. Detemir
        b. Very long-acting
             i. Degludec

   2. As a pre-meal (prandial) bolus dose to cover the extra requirements after food is absorbed -
        a. Short-acting (regular) insulin
        b. Rapid-acting insulin
             i. Lispro
             ii. Aspart
             iii. Glulisine

   3. As a pre-mixed combination of intermediate-acting and short-acting or rapid-acting insulin

The approximate time of onset, half-life, effective peak, and duration of action of the most used insulins are shown in the table below. There is substantial intra-individual and inter-individual variability in onset and duration of insulin action related to the volume injected, the injection site, injection technique, and multiple other factors; therefore, insulin must be adjusted based on patient response.

Pharmacokinetics of commonly used insulin preparations

(A) Prandial insulin

Insulin type	Onset of action	Effective peak	Approximate duration of action*
Lispro, lispro-aabc, aspart, faster aspart, glulisine¶	15 to 30 minutes	1 to 3 hours	4 to 6 hours
Regular	30 minutes	1.5 to 3.5 hours	8 hours

(B) Basal insulin

Insulin type	Half-life	Effective peak	Approximate duration of action*
NPH	4.4 hours	4 to 6 hours	12 hours
Insulin glargine			
U-100	12 hours	No pronounced peak	20 to >24 hours
U-300	19 hours	No pronounced peak	20 to >24 hours
Insulin detemir	5 to 7 hours	3 to 9 hours	6 to 24 hours◊
Insulin degludec (U-100, U-200)	25 hours	No pronounced peak	>24 hours

Glucose-lowering action may vary considerably in different individuals or within the same individual; the duration of action is dose dependent.

¶ Lispro-aabc and faster aspart have quicker pharmacokinetic profiles than standard lispro and aspart.
◊ At higher doses (≥0.8 units/kg), mean duration of action is longer and less variable (22 to 23 hours).

2) When is insulin indicated as initial therapy in type 2 DM?
Indications for initial treatment with insulin include the following:

1. *Severe hyperglycemia on presentation*
    a. For patients presenting with symptoms (eg, weight loss, polydipsia, polyuria) or severe hyperglycemia with ketonuria, insulin is indicated for initial treatment.
    b. For patients presenting with severe hyperglycemia (FBG >250 mg/dL, random glucose consistently >300 mg/dL, A1C >9 %) but without ketonuria or spontaneous weight loss, insulin is an option (or a glucagon-like peptide 1 receptor agonist), along with metformin (if type 1 diabetes is not likely).

2. *Difficulty distinguishing type of diabetes*
    a. Insulin is indicated for initial treatment in patients in whom it is difficult to distinguish type 1 from type 2 diabetes.
    b. Patients who are initially thought to have type 2 diabetes may actually have type 1 diabetes. Although the peak incidence of type 1 diabetes occurs around the time of puberty, approximately 42 percent of cases present after 30 years of age.

3. *Pancreatic insufficiency*
    a. Insulin is also indicated for patients with secondary diabetes due to pancreatic insufficiency, including from cystic fibrosis, chronic pancreatitis, or after pancreatectomy.
    b.

4. *To eliminate glucotoxicity*

a. **Initial intensive insulin treatment** for two to four weeks may be beneficial in patients with type 2 diabetes and may induce a remission that can last for a year or more. By inducing near-normoglycemia with intensive insulin therapy, both endogenous insulin secretion and insulin sensitivity improve. The improvement in insulin secretion is due to the elimination of the deleterious effects of hyperglycemia on beta cell secretory function; in some patients, it results in better glycemic management that can then be maintained with diet and exercise for many months or even years thereafter. Initial, short-term intensive insulin treatment is not widely used.

3) When is Insulin always indicated?
Insulin is always indicated **for patients presenting with:**
- Symptoms of polyuria and/or polyphagia
- Severe hyperglycemia
    - Fasting plasma glucose >250 mg/dL
    - Random glucose consistently >300 mg/dL
    - A1C >9 percent
- Spontaneous weight loss
- Ketonuria
- In patients in whom it is difficult to distinguish type 1 from type 2 diabetes.

4) Which are the rapid acting insulins?
Rapid-acting insulins have a short duration of action and are appropriate for use before meals or when blood glucose levels exceed target levels and correction doses are needed. These agents are associated with less hypoglycemia than regular insulin.

Insulin aspart **has a short onset of action of 5-15 minutes and a short duration of action of 3-5 hours. The peak effect occurs within 30-90 minutes.**

Fiasp also has a rapid onset of action, within 15-20 minutes. The peak effect occurs within 90-130 minutes, and the usual duration of action is 5-7 hours.

Insulin glulisine has a rapid onset of action of 5-15 minutes and a short duration of action of 3-5 hours. The peak effect occurs within 30-90 minutes.

Insulin lispro has a rapid onset of action of 5-15 minutes and a short duration of action of 4 hours.

Orally inhaled rapid-acting insulin is in powder form. When 8 units are administered, maximum serum insulin concentration is reached by 12-15 minutes and declines to baseline by about 180 minutes.

5) Which are the short-acting insulins?
Short-acting insulins are used when a slower onset of action or a longer duration of action is desired.

Regular insulin has a rapid onset of action of 0.5-1 hours and duration of action of 4-6 hours. The peak effects are seen within 2-4 hours. Preparations that contain a mixture of 70% neutral protamine Hagedorn (NPH) and 30% regular human insulin are also available.

6) Which are the intermediate-acting insulins?
Intermediate-acting insulins have a slow onset of action and a longer duration of action. They are commonly combined with faster-acting insulins to maximize the benefits of a single injection.

Insulin neutral protamine Hagedorn (NPH) has an onset of action of 3-4 hours. The peak effect occurs within 8-14 hours, and its usual duration of action is 16-24 hours. The drug appears cloudy and must be gently mixed and checked for clumping; if clumping occurs, the insulin should be discarded.

7) Which are long-acting insulins?

These insulins provide a longer duration of action, and, when combined with rapid- or short-acting insulins, they provide better glucose control.

Insulin detemir is indicated for once- or twice-daily dosing in patients with type 1 or 2 diabetes mellitus. The duration of action is up to 24 hours, the result of slow systemic absorption of detemir from the injection site.

Insulin glargine has no pronounced peaks of action, because a small amount of insulin is gradually released at a constant rate over 24 hours.

Insulin degludec is ultralong-acting insulin. It is highly protein bound, and following SC, the protein-binding provides a depot effect. The elimination half-life is 25 hours, and its duration of action is beyond 42 hours. It is indicated to improve glycemic control in adults with diabetes mellitus who require basal insulin.

Detemir, glargine, and degludec cannot be mixed with rapid-acting insulin.

8) What is the role of long-acting insulins in the treatment of type 2 DM?
- Long-acting insulins include insulin glargine and insulin detemir.

- Insulin glargine has no peak and produces a relatively stable level lasting more than 24 hours. In some patients, it can produce a stable basal serum insulin concentration with a single daily injection; patients requiring lower doses typically are given twice-daily injections.

- Insulin detemir has a duration of action that may be substantially shorter than that of insulin glargine but longer than those of intermediate-acting insulins.

- Degludec is a new ultralong-acting basal insulin; it has a duration of action of up to 42 hours. This new basal insulin forms a soluble multi hexamer after subcutaneous injection to provide a depot effect that is long lasting.

9) Which insulin is preferred for initial treatment?
    - For patients who are initiating insulin (in addition to oral agents, in place of oral agents, or as initial treatment), basal insulin is preferred to prandial insulin. Basal insulin will improve nocturnal and fasting blood glucose (FBG); whereas prandial (pre-meal) bolus insulin will decrease postprandial glucose elevations.
    - Initiation of insulin therapy with a basal insulin has the advantage of convenience in patients who are using insulin for the first time. Basal insulin is associated with greater patient satisfaction and less frequent hypoglycemia
    - Basal and prandial insulins are similarly effective in improving A1C.
    - The type of insulin regimen (basal or prandial) does not affect cardiovascular outcomes. Whether a basal or a prandial strategy is more effective in improving microvascular complications remains uncertain.

10) What is the initial dose for basal insulin?
    - The initial dose for basal insulin (NPH, detemir, glargine, or degludec) is 0.2 units per kg (minimum 10 units, up to 15 to 20 units) subcutaneously daily.
    - If FBG levels are very elevated (>250 mg/dL), A1C is >8 percent, or if a patient is known to be very insulin resistant, initial doses of basal insulin can be higher (eg, 0.3 units per kg or up to 15 to 20 units daily as an initial dose).
    - Subsequent modifications can be made according to daily measurement of FBG and every three-month measurement of A1C.
    - Target FBG is 80 to 130 mg/dL in young patients; higher FBG targets are reasonable for older patients and for those at risk of hypoglycemia.

11) When is basal insulin best given?

Insulin neutral protamine Hagedorn (NPH) or detemir is given at bedtime. Insulin glargine or degludec can be administered any time of day (based on patient preference). Both are reasonable initial regimens.

12) Which basal insulin has the best glycemic efficacy?

The basal insulin preparations (NPH, detemir, glargine, or degludec) do not differ significantly in glycemic efficacy. All types of basal insulin cause similar improvements in A1C. NPH is the cheapest.

13) Is basal insulin alone adequate for glycemic management in type 2 DM?

For many patients with type 2 diabetes, basal insulin alone is often adequate for glycemic management; it reduces glucose toxicity, thereby increasing endogenous insulin secretion, which is sufficient for postprandial excursions.

14) How will you manage persistent fasting hyperglycemia?

If the mean FBG is above target (typically 130 mg/dL), an increase of 2 to 4 units in the basal insulin dose should be made periodically (every three days). In this way, titrate the basal insulin dose over several weeks or months. If FBG levels are very elevated (>250 mg/dL) or if a patient is known to be very insulin resistant, titration can be more aggressive.

As patients approach the glycemic target, it may be helpful to check a mid-sleep blood glucose to rule out hypoglycemia (this can be done when the patient spontaneously wakes overnight).

15) When is pre-meal insulin added to basal insulin?

Patients with persistently elevated A1C despite fasting blood glucose in the target range or people on very high doses of insulin may require rapid-acting pre-meal insulin (similar to treatment for type 1 diabetes). Pre-meal insulin regimens require self-monitoring of glucose levels (ie, before meals) in addition to fasting levels to determine and adjust preprandial dosing.

16) Which is the best prandial (related to a meal) insulin for type 2 diabetes?
- For patients with type 2 diabetes who require prandial insulin, either short (regular) or rapid-acting insulin can be given.
- Rapid-acting insulin is given *immediately before* meals.
- Short-acting (regular) insulin has to be given *30 to 45 minutes before* the meal.

The ability to inject the rapid-acting insulins immediately before meals (as opposed to the 30 to 45 minutes before the meal recommended for short-acting insulins) provides improved convenience for patients. The main reason is that many patients do not take their food within 45 minutes, putting themselves at risk for hypoglycemia. There is little glycemic advantage of analog compared with regular insulin in type 2 diabetes.

17) Which is most effective in lowering postprandial glucose in type 2 DM?

For lowering postprandial glucose, premixed insulin analogues are more effective than either long-acting insulin analogues alone or premixed neutral protamine Hagedorn (NPH)/regular human insulin 70/30.

For lowering HbA1c, premixed insulin analogues are as effective as premixed NPH/regular human insulin 70/30 and more effective than long-acting insulin analogues

The frequency of hypoglycemia reported with premixed insulin analogues is similar to that with premixed human insulin and higher than that with oral antidiabetic agents.

18) What is the role of insulin aspart/Fiasp in the treatment of type 2 DM?
- Fiasp 100IU/ml Penfill is a fast-acting insulin that can lower blood sugar levels after meals. This human insulin analog is formulated with niacinamide, which aids in speeding the initial absorption of insulin.

- It should be taken 15 minutes before a meal or within 20 minutes after starting a meal. Fiasp can be detected in the circulation about 2.5 minutes after it is administered.

- Maximum insulin levels occur approximately 60 minutes after administration.
- Fiasp is usually prescribed along with a long-acting type of insulin.

19) Where is the preferred site for administration of insulin injections in type 2 DM?

All insulin injections should preferably be administered in the abdomen, although they can also be given in the thigh, hip, or buttock regions.

20) What are the disadvantages of insulin therapy?

The major drawbacks associated with insulin therapy in type 2 diabetes are weight gain and hypoglycemia. Glycemic targets may need to be relaxed to reduce the risk of hypoglycemia and/or insulin-associated weight gain.

21) Is combining oral hypoglycemic drug and insulin useful?
- Yes. Using glucose-lowering medications with different mechanisms of action may achieve glucose targets while minimizing total insulin requirements and weight gain. Metformin is often continued with the addition of insulin.

- GLP-1 receptor agonists, DPP-4 inhibitors, and SGLT2 inhibitors can also be continued when insulin is added, although the advantages of doing so must be balanced against increased cost.

- Sulfonylureas, meglitinides, and pioglitazone are usually tapered and stopped when starting insulin, especially prandial insulin, due to reduced efficacy and adverse effects.

22) A type 2 diabetic obese patient has persistent elevation in A1C with FBG in target range. How will you manage?

For patients with persistently elevated glycated hemoglobin levels who have fasting blood glucose (FBG) levels in the target range (80 to 130 mg/dL, or higher, depending on the individualized glycemic target), advise the patient to check finger stick capillary glucose levels fasting, pre-lunch, pre-dinner, and before bed and adjust the prandial insulin regimen accordingly. Prandial insulin is often started as a single injection before the largest meal of the day. Short-term monitoring with continuous glucose monitoring for two weeks may also be helpful in insulin dose adjustment.

If A1C values remain above the desired target despite insulin adjustments, review diet and exercise patterns. In general, inadequate dosing, dietary indiscretion, and/or mismatch of food and insulin dose are the causes of failure of many insulin regimens.

When the dose is >80 units daily, absorption kinetics (which are proportional to volume injected) may be altered. In this setting, administer basal insulin in divided doses twice daily.

23) What is the indication for pramlintide in the treatment of type 1 or type 2 diabetes?

Pramlintide is a synthetic analogue of human amylin, a naturally occurring hormone made in pancreatic beta cells. It slows gastric emptying, suppresses postprandial glucagon secretion, and regulates food intake because of centrally mediated appetite modulation.

Pramlintide is indicated for the treatment of type 1 or type 2 diabetes in combination with insulin. It is administered before mealtime in patients who have not achieved desired glucose control despite optimal insulin therapy. It helps to achieve lower blood glucose levels after meals, less fluctuation of blood glucose levels during the day, and improvement of long-term control of HbA1C levels, compared with insulin alone. Additionally, less insulin use and a reduction in body weight are observed.

Practice points (26)

1) What is the HbA1c target in type 2 DM?
Goals should be tailored to the individual patient and should take the following considerations into account:
- The patient's preferences
- Risk for complications from diabetes
- Comorbidity
- Life expectancy

Aim to achieve an HbA1c level between 7% and 8% in most patients with type 2 diabetes. This higher target is aimed at avoiding the adverse effects (hypoglycemia and weight gain). Risk for hypoglycemia and cost are the main limiting factors in achieving the lowest possible HbA1c.

In elderly patients who have a life expectancy of less than 5 years or in any patient with a terminal disease, tight control may be unnecessary. Patients with cardiovascular or cerebrovascular disease may also need higher preprandial blood glucose targets (eg, 100-150 mg/dL) to prevent severe hypoglycemia.

2) What are the desired goals of glucose values in type 2 DM?
For patients trying to achieve near euglycemia (healthy young and middle-aged adults), premeal glucose values of 80-120 mg/dL are the goal; a value at least 100 mg/dL is desirable when the patient is going to sleep at night.

In patients with less stringent glycemic goals (eg, because of advanced age, advanced complications, or severe concomitant disease), preprandial glucose values of 100-140 mg/dL are desired. Essentially no patient is able to achieve these goals all the time if insulin is needed to treat their disease.

The goal of a combined daytime oral agent plus once-a-day insulin is to lower the fasting glucose level to 100 mg/dL by titrating the insulin. When this target is achieved, the oral agents can be effective in maintaining preprandial and postprandial blood glucose levels throughout the day.

If combined oral agents and insulin fails to lower glucose levels into the normal range, patients should be switched to a daily multiple-injection schedule with a premeal rapid-acting insulin and a longer-acting basal insulin.

3) How should blood glucose levels be managed in type 2 DM?

Ideally, blood glucose should be maintained at near-normal levels (preprandial levels of 90-130 mg/dL and HbA1c levels < 7%). However, focus on glucose alone does not provide adequate treatment for patients with diabetes mellitus. Treatment involves multiple goals (ie, glycemia, lipids, blood pressure).

Aggressive glucose lowering may not be the best strategy in all patients. Individual risk stratification is highly recommended.

4) When will you start initial pharmacologic therapy?
- Early institution of treatment for diabetes, at a time when the A1C is not substantially elevated, is associated with improved glycemic management over time and decreased long-term complications. Pharmacologic therapy (eg, metformin) should be initiated along with lifestyle modification (diet and exercise).
- For most patients presenting with A1C of 7.5 - 8%, pharmacologic therapy should be initiated at the time of type 2 diabetes diagnosis (with lifestyle modification).
- For highly motivated patients with A1C <7.5%, a three- to six-month trial of lifestyle modification before initiating pharmacologic therapy is reasonable.

5) How will you make the choice of initial drug therapy?

In selecting initial therapy, consider the following-
- Presence or absence of symptoms of hyperglycemia
- Baseline A1C level
- Comorbidities
- Individualized treatment goals and preferences

- Glucose-lowering efficacy of individual drugs, adverse effects, and cost.

6) What is the easiest way to correct fasting hyperglycemia in type 2 DM?

In patients with type 2 diabetes, particularly those who have central obesity and hepatic steatosis, the highest preprandial glucose level of the day is before breakfast (because of disordered hepatic glucose production overnight); there is a "stair-step" decrease during the day after the usual post meal rise.

For patients who primarily have fasting hyperglycemia, basal insulin is the easiest way to correct this abnormality (by suppressing hepatic gluconeogenesis). Basal insulin is typically scheduled at bedtime but can be given at suppertime if that is more convenient for the patient.

7) A patient on basal insulin has raised pre-lunch glucose with HbA1c 8%. How will you correct it?

Add rapid acting insulin at breakfast. Insulin regimens should be designed taking lifestyle and meal schedules into account. Premixed insulins are not recommended during adjustment of doses; however, they can be used conveniently, usually before breakfast and/or dinner if the proportion of rapid-acting and intermediate-acting insulins is similar to the fixed proportions available.

8) A patient on basal insulin has raised pre-dinner glucose with HbA1c 8%. How will you correct it?

Add NPH insulin at breakfast or rapid acting insulin at lunch.

9) A patient on basal insulin has raised pre-bed glucose with HbA1c 8%. How will you correct it?

Add rapid acting insulin at dinner.

10) How do you adjust the pre-meal insulin dose?

The optimal dose of pre-meal insulin depends upon current and target blood glucose values, carbohydrate content of the meal, and activity. A typical starting dose is approximately 4 to 6 units or 10 percent of the basal insulin dose. The dose can be increased every three days until the postprandial blood glucose target is achieved. Patients may take a slightly higher dose of prandial insulin for high carbohydrate meals. Prandial insulin dose increases depend on how much prandial insulin the patient is using. As a rule of thumb:

- ≤10 units – Increase by 1 unit
- 11 to 20 units – Increase by 2 units
- >20 units – Increase by 5 units (or more, depending on patient insulin resistance, meal size, and content)

11) What are the advantages and disadvantages of pre-mixed insulin?

Most pre-mixed (biphasic) preparations contain an intermediate-acting insulin and either a short-acting or a rapid-acting insulin. It is suggested not to use pre-mixed insulin initially, because of limited flexibility in adjusting doses. However, pre-mixed insulin is a reasonable option for patients with type 2 diabetes who are doing well on a stable, fixed ratio.

Pre-mixed rapid-acting preparations offer little glycemic advantage compared with adequately titrated basal and bolus insulin.

12) What is the specific glucose value that defines hypoglycemia?

A specific glucose level that defines hypoglycemia has not been identified, as the glycemic thresholds that induce symptoms (and counterregulatory responses) vary within and between individuals. The lower limit of the normal fasting plasma glucose value is 70 mg/dL. A glucose level of <54 mg/dL has been proposed as sufficiently low to indicate serious, clinically important biochemical hypoglycemia. This value identifies an unequivocally low glucose level, one that occurs rarely, if at all, in nondiabetic individuals under physiologic conditions and one that should be avoided because of immediate and long-term consequences to the individual.

- Hypoglycemia in type 2 diabetes usually occurs in those getting a sulfonylurea, a meglitinide, or insulin.

- Hypoglycemia is most often reported in patients taking long-acting drugs, such as glyburide (glibenclamide), compared with the shorter-acting glipizide, glimepiride and gliclazide.

13) Which are the antidiabetic drugs that do not usually cause hypoglycemia?
- Metformin
- Alpha-glucosidase inhibitors
- Thiazolidinediones
- GLP-1 receptor agonists
- DPP-4 inhibitors
- SGLT-2 inhibitors

However, these drugs increase the risk if used with insulin or an insulin secretagogue.

14) What is pseudohypoglycemia?
The person with diabetes reports typical symptoms of hypoglycemia but has a measured glucose level >70 mg/dL. Patients with chronically poorly controlled diabetes can experience symptoms of hypoglycemia as glucose levels fall into the physiologic range.
Pseudo hypoglycemia is also used to describe artifactually low plasma or serum glucose concentrations due to continued metabolism of glucose after the sample is drawn; this can occur when the sample tube does not include an inhibitor of glycolysis and when separation of the plasma or serum is delayed.

15) How will you manage recurrent daytime hypoglycemia?
- Check for apparent changes in diet (timing, amount) or activity to account for hypoglycemia.
- If the patient is taking prandial insulin, the dose should be decreased at the appropriate mealtime (eg, reduce breakfast prandial insulin if hypoglycemia occurs between breakfast and lunch).
- If the hypoglycemia is not severe, a typical approach is to decrease the dose based on how much prandial insulin the patient is taking at the relevant mealtime:
  - ≤10 units – Decrease by 2 units

- 11 to 20 units – Decrease by 4 units
- >20 units – Decrease by 6 to 10 units or 50 percent
- If the hypoglycemia is severe, reduce the dose by 20 to 50 percent or discontinue the prandial insulin and reinitiate/re-titrate if needed.
- Patients should be asked about the timing of their prandial insulin dose and have appropriate timing reinforced.
- If the patient is not taking prandial insulin, the dose of basal insulin should be reduced (by 4 units or 10 percent, whichever is greater).
- If hyperglycemia develops after meals (based on self-monitoring of blood glucose), prandial insulin should be added to cover mealtime excursions.

16) How will you manage recurrent episodes of nocturnal hypoglycemia?

The dose of basal insulin should be reduced (bedtime dosing if taken twice daily) by 4 units or 10 percent, whichever is greater. If the patient is taking bedtime NPH, an alternative is to switch to detemir, insulin glargine, or degludec at 80 to 90 percent of the current total daily dose. Insulin glargine, detemir, and degludec produce less symptomatic and nocturnal hypoglycemia with the important disadvantage of high cost.

17) What is the dawn phenomenon in type 2 DM?

The Dawn phenomenon is common in type 2 diabetes; approximately half have the dawn phenomenon. It is defined as a blood glucose increase of over 20 mg/dL occurring at the end of the night.

18) What is the efficacy of intensive therapy for type 2 DM?

Intense treatment significantly lowers the rate of progression of microvascular complications compared to patients receiving standard care. Rates of macrovascular disease are not altered except in obese individuals getting metformin-monotherapy, in whom the risk of myocardial infarction is significantly decreased.

Tight glycemic control (HbA1c < 7% or lower) is valuable for microvascular and macrovascular disease risk reduction in patients with recent-onset disease, no known cardiovascular diseases, and a longer life expectancy. In patients with known cardiovascular disease, a longer duration of diabetes (15 or more years), and a shorter life expectancy, tighter glycemic control is not as beneficial, particularly with regard to cardiovascular disease risk. Intensive glycemic control reduces the risk of microvascular complications, but at the expense of increased risk of hypoglycemia. Episodes of severe hypoglycemia may be particularly harmful in older individuals with poorer glycemic control and existing cardiovascular disease.

19) What is the treatment for diabetes mellitus in the ED when the type is unknown?

When dealing with patients with known diabetes in the emergency department, distinguishing the type of diabetes can be difficult in 2 groups:
 1. patients who are treated with insulin and are young but clinically appear to have type 2 diabetes, and
 2. older patients with late-onset diabetes who nonetheless take insulin and seem to share characteristics of patients with type 1 diabetes. (This latter group is now said to have latent autoimmune diabetes of the adult [LADA]).

When in doubt, the patient should be treated with insulin and glucose levels should be closely monitored. Some adolescents or young adults who present with classic DKA are subsequently found to have type 2 diabetes.

20) A 50-year-old male has fasting plasma glucose 280 mg/dL, random glucose 360 mg/dL, glycated hemoglobin 9.5 percent but without ketonuria or unintentional weight loss. What is the preferred initial therapy?
 - In this setting, insulin or a GLP-1 receptor agonist are the preferred initial therapies.
 - For patients who are injection-averse or cannot afford the expensive GLP-1 receptor agonist, initial therapy with high-dose sulfonylurea is an alternative option and can rapidly reduce hyperglycemia in patients with severe hyperglycemia.

- Insulin should be used in patients who are underweight, are losing weight, or are ketotic despite adequate caloric intake.

21) Which drug is preferred in patients with established cardiovascular disease?

The GLP-1 receptor agonists liraglutide, semaglutide, and dulaglutide have favorable atherosclerotic cardiovascular and renal outcomes, but they are costly.

22) Which drug is preferred in patients with established kidney disease?
   - SGLT2 inhibitors (empagliflozin, canagliflozin, dapagliflozin) reduce progression of diabetic kidney disease.
     o For patients with chronic kidney disease (urine albumin excretion >300 mg/day and estimated glomerular filtration rate <60 but ≥30 mL/min/1.73 m2), prescribe a low dose of an SGLT2 inhibitor.
     o SGLT2 inhibitors are not recommended for initiation with eGFR <30 to 45 mL/min/1.73 m2; they have less glycemic efficacy with eGFR <45 mL/min/1.73 m2.
     o Avoid use of SGLT2 inhibitors in patients with:
       - frequent bacterial urinary tract infections or genitourinary yeast infections,
       - low bone density and high risk for falls and fractures,
       - foot ulceration, and
       - factors predisposing to diabetic ketoacidosis (eg, pancreatic insufficiency, drug, or alcohol abuse disorder).

23) Which drug is preferred in a patient with nondialysis chronic kidney disease stage 4 (eg, eGFR <30 mL/min/1.73 m2)?
   - A short-acting low-dose sulfonylurea (eg, glipizide), repaglinide, linagliptin, insulin or a GLP-1 receptor agonist may be used.
     o Repaglinide is much shorter acting than sulfonylureas and is principally metabolized by the liver, with less than 10 percent renally excreted.

- Linagliptin is the only DPP-4 inhibitor that does not require a dose adjustment in the setting of kidney failure.
- Give a greater portion of insulin during the day due to the risk of nocturnal hypoglycemia.
- GLP-1 receptor agonists may also be used safely in chronic kidney disease stage 4.

24) A diabetic patient with A1C levels of 9% was put on metformin. After 6 months his A1C level is 10%. He cannot tolerate metformin anymore. Which antidiabetic drug would you use?

Ans - Insulin or a GLP-1 receptor agonist.

Insulin is usually used for type 2 diabetes only when inadequate glycemic management persists despite oral agents and lifestyle intervention. There is increasing data to support using insulin earlier and more aggressively in type 2 diabetes. By inducing near normoglycemia with intensive insulin therapy, both endogenous insulin secretion and insulin sensitivity improve; this results in better glycemic management, which can then be maintained with diet, exercise, and oral hypoglycemics for many months thereafter. Insulin may cause weight gain and hypoglycemia.

If weight loss is a priority, a GLP-1 receptor agonist is a reasonable alternative to insulin.

25) A diabetic patient with A1C levels of 9% was put on metformin. After 6 months his A1C level is 8.5%. He cannot tolerate metformin anymore. Which antidiabetic drug would you use?
- For patients with A1C levels <9%, options include sulfonylureas, SGLT2 inhibitors, DPP-4 inhibitors, repaglinide, or pioglitazone (in addition to insulin or GLP-1 receptor agonists).
    - If weight loss is a priority, GLP-1 receptor agonists or SGLT2 inhibitors may be a helpful choice. DPP-4 inhibitors, which are weight neutral, also may be reasonable options.
    - If cost is a concern, a short- or intermediate-acting sulfonylurea, such as glipizide or glimepiride, is a reasonable alternative.

- If avoidance of hypoglycemia is a priority (ie, because of potentially dangerous work), GLP-1 receptor agonists, SGLT2 inhibitors, DPP-4 inhibitors, or pioglitazone are options as they are associated with a low hypoglycemia risk.

26) How does type 2 diabetes affect morbidity and mortality in COVID-19?

Type 2 diabetes is included in the list of conditions that increase the likelihood of severe illness in persons with COVID-19.

Chronic complications and their prevention (27)

1) What factors influence the prognosis of type 2 DM?

The prognosis in patients with diabetes mellitus is strongly influenced by the degree of control of their disease. Chronic hyperglycemia is associated with an increased risk of microvascular complications. Reversion to normal glucose regulation is associated with a better prognosis.

2) What are the guidelines for monitoring complications in type 2 DM?

Initiate monitoring for complications at the time of diagnosis of diabetes mellitus. This should include yearly dilated eye examinations, annual microalbumin checks, and foot examinations at each visit.

3) Which interventions may help prevent or limit the complications of DM?

Approaches to prevention of diabetic complications include the following:

1. HbA1c every 3-6 months
2. Yearly dilated eye examinations
3. Annual microalbumin checks
4. Foot examinations at each visit

5. Blood pressure < 130/80 mm Hg, lower in diabetic nephropathy
6. Statin therapy to reduce low-density lipoprotein cholesterol

4) How do the complications differ by type of DM?
Although the pathophysiology of the disease differs between the types of diabetes, most of the complications, including microvascular, macrovascular, and neuropathic, are similar regardless of the type of diabetes. Hyperglycemia is the determinant of microvascular and metabolic complications. Macrovascular disease may be less related to glycemia.

5) What are the common vascular complications of type 2 DM?
   - Microvascular complications of diabetes include retinal, renal, and possibly neuropathic disease.
   - Macrovascular complications include coronary artery and peripheral vascular disease.

6) What is the effect of glycemic control on the microvascular vascular complications in type 2 DM?
   Improved glycemic control improves the risk of microvascular complications (primarily retinopathy, nephropathy) in patients with type 2 diabetes.

7) What is the effect of glycemic control on the macrovascular vascular complications in type 2 DM?
   - Most clinical trials have not demonstrated a beneficial effect of intensive therapy on macrovascular outcomes in type 2 diabetes.
     o Intensive treatment of blood glucose is associated with an increased risk of hypoglycemia, as well as additional side effects, and cost.
     o Depending on the agents prescribed, weight gain may also occur with intensive treatment.
   - Initial intensive control (A1C 7 percent) in individuals with newly diagnosed diabetes may have long-term benefits in decreasing the risk of myocardial infarction, diabetes-related death, and overall death.

8) What is the most effective approach for prevention of macrovascular complications in type 2 DM?

The most effective approach for prevention of macrovascular complications is multifactorial risk factor reduction-
- glycemic control,
- stopping smoking,
- aggressive blood pressure control,
- treatment of dyslipidemia, and,
- daily aspirin, for secondary prevention.

9) What is the risk of coronary heart disease in adults with type 2 DM?

Men with diabetes face a 2-fold increased risk for CHD, and women have a 3- to 4-fold increased risk. Cardiovascular disease is the major source of mortality in patients with type 2 diabetes mellitus. Approximately two thirds of people with diabetes die of heart disease or stroke.

Control of conventional risk factors is more important than glycemic control. Control of hypertension, aspirin therapy, and lowering of LDL cholesterol levels are vitally important in reducing CHD risk.

10) When does cardiovascular risk increase in type 2 DM?

Increased macrovascular risk begins prior to the development of frank hyperglycemia, presumably with the onset of insulin resistance; the risk for microvascular risk begins at the onset of hyperglycemia.

11) Which lipid abnormalities contribute to cardiovascular risk in type 2 DM?

Cardiovascular risk in people with diabetes is related in part to insulin resistance, with the following concomitant lipid abnormalities:

- Elevated levels of small, dense low-density lipoprotein (LDL) cholesterol particles

- Low levels of high-density lipoprotein (HDL) cholesterol

- Elevated levels of triglyceride-rich remnant lipoproteins

Thrombotic abnormalities (ie, elevated type-1 plasminogen activator inhibitor [PAI-1], elevated fibrinogen) and hypertension are also involved. Other conventional atherosclerotic risk factors (eg, family history, smoking, elevated LDL cholesterol) also affect cardiovascular risk.

12) What are the guidelines for the use of statins in type 2 DM?
Dyslipidemia is common in patients with type 2 diabetes mellitus and often takes the form of high triglyceride and low HDL cholesterol levels. Statins are effective for primary and secondary prevention of coronary heart disease in patients with diabetes.

The American Diabetes Association (ADA) recommends statin use for nearly everyone with diabetes. The ADA guidelines divide diabetes patients by 3 age groups:

Younger than 40 years:
- No statins for those with no cardiovascular disease risk factors other than diabetes.
- Moderate intensity or high-intensity statin doses for those with additional CVD risk factors (baseline LDL cholesterol 100 or greater, high blood pressure, smoking, and overweight/obesity)
- High-intensity statin doses for those with overt CVD (including previous cardiovascular events or acute coronary syndrome).

Age 40-75 years:
- Moderate-intensity statins for those with no additional risk factors
- High-intensity statins for those with either CVD risk factors or overt CVD.

Older than 75 years:
- Moderate-intensity statins for those with CVD risk factors
- High-intensity statins for those with overt CVD.

Lipid monitoring for adherence is recommended as needed; annual monitoring is advised for patients younger than 40 years who have not yet started on statins.

13) What are the guidelines on cardiovascular disease management and prevention in patients with diabetes or prediabetes?

Patient CV risk is classified as follows:

- Medium CV risk
    - Young patients without other CV risk factors who have had diabetes for less than 10 years

- High CV risk
    - Patients who lack target-organ damage but have had diabetes for over 10 years and in whom at least one other risk factor exists

- Very high CV risk
    - Patients with CVD or target-organ damage or in whom type 1 diabetes has been present for more than 20 years

The recommendations include the following:
- In drug-naïve patients with type 2 diabetes and established CVD, administration of SGLT-2 inhibitor or GLP-1 receptor agonist should be immediately initiated or added to existing metformin treatment
- Aspirin should be used in high- and very high–risk patients (on an individual basis) but not in moderate-risk patients
- Very high–risk patients in whom LDL cholesterol levels are persistently high even with maximal statin and ezetimibe therapy or who have statin intolerance should undergo proprotein convertase subtilisin/kexin type 9 (PCSK-9) inhibitor treatment
- An HbA1c level of under 7% is advised, particularly in young adults who have had diabetes for only a short time

14) What blood pressure goals are recommended for type 2 DM?

Hypertension increases microvascular and macrovascular risk in patients with diabetes mellitus. The goal in most patients with diabetes and hypertension should be a systolic blood pressure below 140 mm Hg and a diastolic blood pressure under 90 mm Hg. For patients with a high risk of cardiovascular disease, however, it may be appropriate to target a lower SBP/DBP (below 130/80 mm Hg), if the goal can be met "without undue treatment burden."

Blood pressure should be measured at every routine clinical care visit. Patients whose blood pressure is at, or above 140/90 mm Hg, should undergo multiple readings to confirm hypertension, including blood pressure assessment on a separate day.

15) Which antihypertensive medications are recommended for type 2 DM?

ACE inhibitors or ARBs are preferred because of their proven renal protection effects in patients with diabetes. Many patients require multiple agents. Diuretics or calcium channel blockers frequently are useful as second and third agents.

16) When and how should screening for microalbuminuria be performed in patients with type 2 DM?

Normal urine albumin excretion is less than 30 mg daily; microalbuminuria is defined as 30-300 mg daily (20-200 mcg/min). Because of wide variability among patients, microalbuminuria should be found on at least 2 of 3 samples over 3-6 months. Higher values can be detected by standard protein dipstick screening and are considered microproteinuria.

Annual screening for microalbuminuria is recommended in all patients with diabetes. Measuring the albumin-to-creatinine ratio in a spot urine sample is the easiest method; the ratio, expressed in mg/g, is equivalent to albumin excretion in milligrams daily. A result greater than 30 mg/g indicates albuminuria, in which case a quantitation on a timed urine specimen (ie, overnight, 10 h, or 24 h) should be performed.

17) What does microalbuminuria indicate in type 2 DM and how does it differ from type 1 DM?

In type 1 diabetes mellitus, microalbuminuria is a good indicator of early kidney damage. In type 2 diabetes mellitus, microalbuminuria is a common finding (even at diagnosis) and is a risk factor for macrovascular (especially coronary heart) disease. It is a weaker predictor of future kidney disease in type 2 diabetes mellitus.

18) What are the ophthalmologic complications of type 2 DM?

Diabetes can affect the lens, vitreous, and retina. Visual blurring may develop acutely as the lens changes shape with marked changes in blood glucose concentrations. This effect, which is caused by osmotic fluxes of water into and out of the lens, usually occurs as hyperglycemia increases, but it also may be seen when high glucose levels are lowered rapidly. In either case, recovery to baseline visual acuity can take up to a month.

Patients with diabetes also tend to develop senile cataracts sooner than persons without diabetes. Development of senile cataracts is not related to the degree of glycemic control, however.

19) What are the treatment options for neuropathy in type 2 diabetes mellitus (DM)?

Peripheral neuropathy is the most common complication observed in patients with type 2 diabetes in outpatient clinics. Patients may have paresthesias, numbness, or pain. The feet are involved more often than the hands.

Improved glycemic control early may alleviate some of the symptoms, although sometimes symptoms actually worsen with lowering of blood glucose levels. Later symptomatic therapy largely is empirical and may include the following:

- Low-dose tricyclic antidepressants

- Duloxetine

- Anticonvulsants (eg, phenytoin, gabapentin, carbamazepine)

- Topical capsaicin

- Various pain medications, including NSAIDs

Protection of the feet by applying lubricating agents (but not between the toes) and wearing appropriate footwear (shoes and socks or stockings) is important. Daily inspection of the feet after bathing is mandatory.

20) How does autonomic neuropathy manifest in type 2 DM?

Autonomic neuropathy may manifest as orthostatic hypotension. Such patients may require volume expanders or adrenergic agents. Patients with cystopathy may benefit from cholinergic agents.

21) What are the acute-onset mononeuropathies caused by type 2 DM?

Acute-onset mononeuropathies in diabetes include acute cranial mononeuropathies, mononeuropathy multiplex, focal lesions of the brachial or lumbosacral plexus, and radiculopathies.

22) What are the treatment options for gastroparesis in type 2 DM?

Gastroparesis is usually less of a problem in patients with type 2 diabetes mellitus than in those with type 1. Improved glycemic control, discontinuation of medications that slow gastric motility, and the use of metoclopramide may be helpful. Metoclopramide use preferably should be limited to a few days at a time; long-term use has been linked to tardive dyskinesia.

23) Which infectious diseases are increased in type 2 DM?

Diabetes increases susceptibility to various types of infections. The most common sites of infection in diabetic patients are the skin and urinary tract. Patients with diabetes have an increased risk of asymptomatic bacteriuria and pyuria, cystitis, and serious upper urinary tract infection.

Sensory neuropathy, atherosclerotic vascular disease, and hyperglycemia all predispose patients with diabetes to skin and soft tissue infections. These can affect any skin surface but most commonly involve the feet. Dermatologic infections that occur with increased frequency in patients with diabetes include staphylococcal follicular skin infections, superficial fungal infections, cellulitis, erysipelas, and oral or genital candidal infections.

Bullosis diabeticorum is a spontaneous, noninflammatory, blistering condition of acral skin that is unique to patients with diabetes mellitus. Blisters in this disease typically heal spontaneously, within 2-6 weeks, but secondary infection may develop.

Contiguous spread of a polymicrobial infection from a skin ulcer (particularly a chronic ulcer) to adjacent bone is common in patients with diabetes.

Malignant otitis externa, rhinocerebral mucormycosis, and emphysematous pyelonephritis, occur almost exclusively in patients with diabetes. Malignant or necrotizing otitis externa principally occurs in diabetic patients older than 35 years and is almost always due to Pseudomonas aeruginosa. Patients typically present with severe ear pain and otorrhea.

Rhinocerebral mucormycosis refers to infections caused by various ubiquitous molds. Invasive disease occurs in patients with poorly controlled diabetes, especially those with diabetic ketoacidosis. Organisms colonize the nose and paranasal sinuses, spreading to adjacent tissues by invading blood vessels and causing soft tissue necrosis and bony erosion.

24) How is serious intercurrent medical illness in type 2 DM managed?
Patients with intercurrent illness become more insulin resistant because of the effects of increased counterregulatory (ie, anti-insulin) hormones. Therefore, despite decreased nutritional intake, glycemia may worsen.

Patients on oral agents may need transient therapy with insulin to achieve adequate glycemic control. If patients taking metformin have any illness that leads to dehydration or hypoperfusion, the drug should be temporarily discontinued because of a possible increased risk of lactic acidosis.

25) What are the criteria for testing for diabetes or prediabetes in asymptomatic adults?

Criteria for testing for diabetes or prediabetes in asymptomatic adults

1. Testing should be considered in overweight or obese (BMI ≥23 kg/m² in Asians) adults who have one or more of the following risk factors:
   - First-degree relative with diabetes
   - History of CVD
   - Hypertension (≥140/90 mmHg or on therapy for hypertension)
   - HDL cholesterol level <35 mg/dL and/or a triglyceride level >250 mg/dL
   - Women with polycystic ovary syndrome
   - Physical inactivity
   - Other clinical conditions associated with insulin resistance (eg, severe obesity, acanthosis nigricans)
2. Patients with prediabetes (A1C ≥5.7%, IGT, or IFG) should be tested yearly.
3. Women who were diagnosed with GDM should have lifelong testing at least every 3 years.
4. For all other patients, testing should begin at age 45 years.
5. If results are normal, testing should be repeated at a minimum of 3-year intervals, with consideration of more frequent testing depending on initial results and risk status.

Exercise and weight loss successfully decreases the development of diabetes.

26) What is the role of metformin in prediabetes?

In addition to lifestyle counseling, metformin is considered in selected patients with prediabetes as follows:

- Obesity

- Age younger than 60 years

- Both impaired fasting glucose and impaired glucose tolerance

- Other risk factors present
  - HbA1C >6%
  - Hypertension
  - Low HDL cholesterol
  - Elevated triglycerides
  - Family history of diabetes in a first-degree relative.

27) What can be done for the primary prevention of stroke in patients with type 2 DM?

Guidelines for the primary prevention of stroke include the following recommendations for patients with diabetes:

- Physical activity (30 minutes or more of moderate-intensity activity on a daily basis)

- Regular blood pressure screening

- A low-sodium, high-potassium diet to reduce blood pressure

- A blood pressure goal of less than 130/80 mm Hg

- Drug therapy with ACE inhibitors or ARBs

- A diet emphasizing consumption of fruits, vegetables, and low-fat dairy products (may lower stroke risk)

- Statin therapy, especially in patients with other risk factors; monotherapy with fibrates may also be considered to lower stroke risk

The benefit of taking aspirin for the reduction of stroke risk has not been fully demonstrated in diabetic patients.

DIABETIC KETOACIDOSIS (DKA) (86)

Etiopathogenesis (14)

1) What are the 3 important features of DKA?
The 3 important features of DKA are:
  1. hyperglycemia,
  2. ketoacidosis, and
  3. ketonuria.

- DKA is caused by absolute or relative insulin deficiency accompanied by an increase in counter-regulatory hormones (ie, glucagon, cortisol, growth hormone, epinephrine). This type of hormonal imbalance enhances:
  - hepatic gluconeogenesis,
  - glycogenolysis, and
  - lipolysis.
- Insulin deficiency inhibits the ability of glucose to enter cells for utilization as fuel.
  - When glucose utilization is impaired because of insulin deficiency, energy must be obtained from fatty acid metabolism. Therefore, the liver rapidly breaks down fat into ketones to use as a fuel source.
  - The overproduction of ketones results, causing them to accumulate in the blood and urine and turn the blood acidic.
- DKA occurs mainly in patients with type 1 diabetes, but it is not uncommon in some patients with type 2 diabetes.

2) What are the two hormonal abnormalities responsible for the development of DKA?

Two hormonal abnormalities are largely responsible for the development of DKA in patients with uncontrolled diabetes are:
1. Insulin deficiency and/or resistance.
    a. The deficiency in insulin is either absolute deficiency, or a relative deficiency caused by excess counterregulatory hormones
2. Glucagon excess, which results from removal of the normal suppressive effect of insulin. Although glucagon excess contributes to the development of DKA, it is not essential.

3) What causes increased Ketone production in DKA?

Both insulin deficiency and glucagon excess contribute to the genesis of DKA. However, glucagon is contributory, but not essential, for DKA to occur.

Insulin deficiency will cause enhanced lipolysis from peripheral fat stores, which releases free fatty acids and glycerol. The fatty acids are taken up by hepatocytes where ketone bodies (acetoacetic acid, beta-hydroxybutyric acid, and acetone) are synthesized because of the low insulin and high glucagon activity. Ketones provide an alternate water-soluble source of energy when glucose availability is reduced.

Within the hepatocyte cytoplasm, they are "activated" by linkage of the fatty acid to coenzyme A (CoA), forming acyl-CoA (ie, fatty acid-CoA). The combination of low insulin and increased glucagon activity in the liver cells creates conditions that accelerate the entry of the acyl-CoA into the mitochondria. This transport is mediated by a pair of carnitines palmityl transferase reactions

4) Which are the other hormones that contribute to the development of DKA?

In addition to the two primary hormones mentioned above, increased secretion of catecholamines, cortisol, and growth hormone also contribute to the increases in glucose and ketoacid production (these hormones oppose the actions of insulin).

5) What causes hyperglycemia in DKA?
   - When there is insulin deficiency, muscle, fat, and liver do not take up glucose.
   - Counterregulatory hormones, such as glucagon, growth hormone, and catecholamines, enhance triglyceride breakdown into free fatty acids and gluconeogenesis. This is the main cause for the elevation in serum glucose level in DKA.
     - The hyperglycemia causes osmotic diuresis resulting in depletion of water sodium, potassium, and phosphates.
   - Beta-oxidation of these free fatty acids leads to increased formation of ketone bodies.
     - Metabolic acidosis results.

6) What is the role of hepatic gluconeogenesis and glycogenolysis in the pathogenesis of DKA?
   - Insulin deficiency and counter-regulatory hormone excess causes hepatic gluconeogenesis and glycogenolysis resulting in severe hyperglycemia.
   - In addition, the decreased glucose uptake by peripheral tissues due to insulin deficiency aggravates the hyperglycemia.
   - Increased proteolysis and decreased protein synthesis as result of insulin deficiency add more gluconeogenic substrates to the gluconeogenesis process.

7) What is the role of lipolysis in the pathogenesis of DKA?
   - Liver metabolizes free fatty acids as an alternative energy source (ie, ketogenesis) results in accumulation of ketones (acetone) and ketoacids (acetoacetic acid).
   - Metabolism in DKA shifts from the normal state characterized by carbohydrate metabolism to a starvation state characterized by fat metabolism.

8) What causes dehydration in DKA?
   - Hyperglycemia results in glucosuria
     - Glucosuria causes osmotic diuresis and water loss in the urine.

- Increased water loss results in severe dehydration, thirst, tissue hypoperfusion, and, possibly, lactic acidosis, or renal impairment.

9) How much is the free water loss in DKA?
   - Typical free water loss in DKA is approximately 6 liters (100 mL/kg of body weight).
     - The initial half of this amount is derived from intracellular fluid and precedes signs of dehydration
     - The other half is from extracellular fluid and is responsible for signs of dehydration. See table below.

Typical total body deficits of water and electrolytes in DKA

	DKA	HHS
Total water (L)	6	9
Water (mL/kg)	100	100 to 200
Na$^+$ (mEq/kg)	7 to 10	5 to 13
Cl$^-$ (mEq/kg)	3 to 5	5 to 15
K$^+$ (mEq/kg)	3 to 5	4 to 6
PO$_4$ (mmol/kg)	5 to 7	3 to 7
Mg^{++} (mEq/kg)	1 to 2	1 to 2
Ca^{++} (mEq/kg)	1 to 2	1 to 2

10) What is the overall electrolyte loss in DKA?

Typical overall electrolyte loss includes:
- 200-500 mEq/L of potassium,
- 300-700 mEq/L of sodium, and
- 350-500 mEq/L of chloride.

The combined effects of serum hyperosmolarity, dehydration, and acidosis result in increased osmolarity in brain cells that clinically manifests as an alteration in the level of consciousness.

11) What causes potassium loss in DKA?
- Patients presenting with DKA have a potassium deficit of 300 to 600 mEq.
    - Potassium loss is caused by a shift of potassium from the intracellular to the extracellular space in an exchange with hydrogen ions that accumulate extracellularly in acidosis.
    - Much of the shifted extracellular potassium is lost in urine because of osmotic diuresis (increased urinary losses due to the glucose osmotic diuresis).
- **_Despite these large total body potassium deficits, the serum potassium concentration is usually normal or, in one-third of patients, elevated on admission._**
    - A normal or even elevated serum potassium concentration may be seen due to the extracellular shift of potassium.
        - Potassium is carried across the cell membrane with water (this process is called solvent drag)
        - Acidemia per se plays a small role in the shift of potassium from the ICF to the ECF in patients with DKA.
    - Patients with initial hypokalemia have severe and serious total body potassium depletion.
    - The serum potassium concentration can drop precipitously once insulin treatment is started.
        - Insulin promotes potassium uptake by the cells.
        - Take great care to repeatedly monitor serum potassium levels.

12) What percent of patients with DKA presents with low serum potassium levels?
- Patients presenting with DKA have a potassium deficit that averages 300 to 600 mEq. Despite total body potassium deficits, hypokalemia is observed in only approximately 5 percent of cases.
- The serum potassium concentration is usually normal or, in one-third of patients, elevated on admission. This is due to a shift of potassium from intracellular fluid to extracellular fluid caused by hyperosmolality and insulin deficiency.
    - Insulin therapy shifts potassium into cells and lowers the potassium concentration. This may cause severe hypokalemia, particularly in patients who present with a normal or low serum potassium concentration.
    - Careful monitoring and timely administration of potassium supplementation are essential.

13) What causes sodium loss in DKA?
- Most patients with DKA are mildly hyponatremic.
    - The measured serum Na concentration in DKA is variable because of the interaction of multiple factors, some that lower Na concentration and others that raise it.
- Sodium is lost in the urine during the osmotic diuresis.
- High serum osmolarity created by hyperglycemia pulls water out of the cells (ie, from intracellular to extracellular space), and this reduces the plasma Na concentration (dilutional hyponatremia).

14) What causes anion gap metabolic acidosis in DKA?
DKA typically presents as an elevated anion gap metabolic acidosis. This is caused by the accumulation of beta-hydroxybutyrate and acetoacetic acids. Serum anion gap = serum sodium - (serum chloride + bicarbonate).

Clinical features (8)

1) When does DKA develop in type 2 diabetes?

DKA is characteristically associated with type 1 diabetes. It also occurs in type 2 diabetes under conditions of extreme stress such as:
- serious infection,
- trauma,
- cardiovascular or other emergencies, and,
- less often, as a presenting manifestation of type 2 diabetes (a disorder called ketosis-prone diabetes mellitus).

2) What is the most common precipitating cause of DKA?
- DKA usually evolves rapidly, over a 24-hour period.
- A precipitating event can usually be identified in patients with DKA
  - The most common precipitating cause of DKA is infection (eg, pneumonia, prostatitis, UTI) - 40%.
  - Missed insulin treatment - 25%.
- Other precipitating causes of DKA in type 2 diabetes mellitus:
  - Intercurrent illness (eg, myocardial infarction, stroke)
  - Medication (eg, corticosteroids, sodium-glucose cotransporter-2 inhibitors)

Predisposing or precipitating factors for DKA

---

1. Inadequate insulin treatment or noncompliance
2. New-onset diabetes (20 to 25 percent) - DKA is a common presentation.
3. Acute illness
    a. Infection (30 to 40 percent)
    b. Cerebral vascular accident
    c. Myocardial infarction
    d. Sepsis
    e. Acute pancreatitis
4. Drugs
    a. Glucocorticoids
    b. Higher-dose thiazide diuretics
    c. Sympathomimetic agents (eg, dobutamine, terbutaline)

d. Clozapine or olanzapine
  e. Cocaine
  f. SGLT2 inhibitors
  g. Lithium

3) What are the most common early symptoms of DKA?
- The most common early symptoms of DKA are the insidious increase in polydipsia (increased thirst) and polyuria.
- The following are other signs and symptoms of DKA:
    - Generalized weakness, and fatigability
    - Nausea, vomiting, and anorexia
    - Abdominal pain (45%)
    - History of failure to comply with insulin therapy or missed insulin injections
    - Altered consciousness (eg, disorientation, confusion, rarely coma)

Clinical features of DKA

- DKA usually evolves rapidly over a 24-hour period.
- Common, early signs of ketoacidosis include:
    - nausea, vomiting,
    - abdominal pain, and
    - hyperventilation.
- The earliest symptoms of marked hyperglycemia are:
    - polyuria,
    - polydipsia, and
    - weight loss.
- As hyperglycemia worsens, neurologic symptoms appear and may progress to include lethargy, focal deficits, obtundation, seizure, and coma.
- Common causes of DKA include infection; noncompliance, inappropriate adjustment, or cessation of insulin; new-onset diabetes mellitus; and myocardial ischemia.

4) What are physical findings of diabetic ketoacidosis (DKA)?
   1. Signs of volume depletion
      a. Dry skin (dry axillae)
      b. Dry mucous membranes
      c. Decreased skin turgor
      d. Low jugular venous pressure
      e. Weak and rapid pulse
      f. Hypotension, if severe.
   2. Kussmaul respirations (deep respirations reflecting the compensatory hyperventilation)
   3. Fruity breath odor ((due to exhaled acetone).

Evaluation of DKA

- Assess vital signs, cardiorespiratory status, and mental status.
- Assess volume status: vital signs, skin turgor, mucosa, urine output.
- Search for signs of infection in all cases.
- Look for signs of precipitating intercurrent illnesses such as MI, UTI, and pneumonia.

5) What are signs of dehydration in DKA?
- Signs of dehydration include:
  - Dry skin (dry axillae)
  - Dry tongue
  - Decreased skin turgor
  - Weak and rapid pulse
  - Low jugular venous pressure
  - Hypotension, if severe.

6) What are signs of acidosis in DKA?
- Signs of acidosis include:
  - Rapid, shallow breathing (sigh breathing)
  - As the acidosis grows more severe, breathing becomes slower, deeper, and labored (air hunger).
  - Disturbance of consciousness.
  - The breath has a fruity smell.

The presence of these signs signifies a severe form of DKA.

7) Why does Kussmaul breathing occur in DKA?
- The most common cause of Kussmaul respirations is DKA, where there is a drop in pH and bicarbonate serum levels. The low serum pH stimulates the respiratory center in the brain stem.
- Kussmaul breathing is a deep, sighing breathing pattern that indicates metabolic acidosis. This respiratory compensatory reduces the PCO2, which tends to lower the hydrogen ion concentration towards normal.
- Initially, in acidosis, the respiratory pattern is rapid and shallow, but as the acidosis progresses, the inspirations become deeper. It is only in the later stages that true Kussmaul respirations are seen.

8) Are mental changes typical in DKA?
- Mental status changes can be seen with mild-to-moderate DKA; more severe deterioration in mental status is typical with moderate-to-severe DKA.
- The combined effects of serum hyperosmolarity, dehydration, and acidosis result in increased osmolarity in brain cells that clinically manifests as an alteration in the level of consciousness.

Lab investigations (24)

1) Which lab studies are performed in DKA?
Initial and repeat laboratory studies for patients with DKA include the following:
1. Serum glucose levels
2. Serum electrolyte levels with calculation of the anion gap (eg, potassium, sodium, chloride, magnesium, calcium, phosphorus)
3. Bicarbonate levels
4. BUN and creatinine levels
5. Complete blood count
6. Urine ketones by dipstick
7. Serum ketone levels (if urine ketones are present)
8. Serum or capillary beta-hydroxybutyrate levels
9. ABG measurements if the serum bicarbonate is substantially reduced, or hypoxia is suspected
10. Plasma osmolality (Posm)

11. ECG

Additional testing, such as cultures of urine, sputum, and blood, serum lipase and amylase, and chest radiograph should be performed on a case-by-case basis. Infection (most commonly pneumonia and urinary tract infection) is a common precipitating event. Thus, cultures should be obtained if there are suggestive clinical findings. Recognize that infection may exist in the absence of fever in these patients

2) When should lab testing in DKA be repeated?

Laboratory studies for DKA should be scheduled as follows:
- Blood tests for glucose every 1-2 h until patient is stable, then every 4-6 h
- Serum electrolyte determinations every 1-2 h until patient is stable, then every 4-6 h
- Initial blood urea nitrogen
- Initial arterial blood gas measurements, followed with bicarbonate as necessary

3) What are the typical lab findings seen in DKA?

DKA is characterized by the triad of:
1. Hyperglycemia
    a. The serum glucose concentration is usually between 350 to 500 mg/dL
    b. < 800 mg/dL (frequently > 1000 mg/dL in HHS)
    c. Glucose level may be mildly elevated or even normal in:
        i. starvation,
        ii. pregnancy,
        iii. treatment with insulin prior to arrival in the emergency department, or
        iv. use of sodium-glucose co-transporter 2 inhibitors.
2. High anion gap metabolic acidosis
    a. Bicarbonate level less than 18 mEq/L,
    b. pH less than 7.30
3. ketonemia and ketonuria.

4) What is the biochemical definition of DKA?
Biochemical definition of DKA
1. Increase in the serum concentration of ketones greater than 5 mEq/L,
2. Blood sugar level greater than 250 mg/dL, and
3. Arterial pH less than 7.3.

Other characteristic abnormalities are-
- Ketonemia and ketonuria
- Serum bicarbonate level of 18 mEq/L or less (less than 5 mEq/L is indicative of severe DKA),
- Increased anion gap,
- Increased serum osmolarity,
- Increased BUN and serum creatinine concentration (due the reduction in glomerular filtration rate induced by hypovolemia), and
- Increased serum uric acid.

5) How are mild, moderate, and severe DKA defined?

Severity	pH	Bicarbonate	Anion gap
Mild DKA	7.25 - 7.3	15 - 18 mEq/L	greater than 10
Moderate DKA	7.2 - 7.24	10 - 15 mEq/L	greater than 12
Severe DKA	less than 7.0	less than 10 mEq/L	greater than 12

These figures differentiate DKA from HHS where blood glucose is greater than 600 mg/dL, but pH is greater than 7.3 and serum bicarbonate greater than 15 mEq/L.

6) What conditions cause euglycemic DKA?
In euglycemic DKA, the serum glucose is normal or near normal. Conditions causing euglycemic DKA are:
- in patients with poor oral intake,

- those treated with insulin prior to arrival in the emergency department,
- in pregnant women, and
- with sodium-glucose co-transporter 2 (SGLT2) inhibitors.
  - o The glycosuria caused by SGLT2 inhibitors can minimize or prevent the development of hyperglycemia, despite very low insulin levels/activity and development of ketoacidosis.

Patients with euglycemic diabetic ketoacidosis require both insulin and glucose to reverse the ketoacidosis.

7) Which is a true keto acid?
   a. Acetoacetic acid
   b. Beta-hydroxybutyric acid
   c. Acetone
   d. All the above

Ans – a
Three ketone bodies are produced and accumulate in DKA.
   1. Acetoacetic acid is the only one that is a true keto acid.
   2. Beta-hydroxybutyric acid is a hydroxyacid formed by the reduction of acetoacetic acid. This is the predominant ketone body present in DKA.
   3. Acetone is derived from the decarboxylation of acetoacetic acid. Acetone is a true ketone, not an acid.

8) Which is the predominant serum ketone body present in DKA?
   - Beta-hydroxybutyric acid is the predominant ketone body present in DKA. It is formed by the reduction of acetoacetic acid.
   - Testing for serum ketones is generally performed if urine testing is positive.
   - Urine ketone bodies are detected with nitroprusside tests.
   - Serum ketones can be detected with either a nitroprusside test or by direct assay of beta-hydroxybutyrate levels.
     - o Direct assay of beta-hydroxybutyrate levels is preferred, particularly for monitoring response to therapy.

9) Is urine testing for ketones necessary to diagnose diabetic ketoacidosis (DKA)?
- Urine dipstick testing with nitroprusside tablets (Acetest) is widely utilized, and results are available within minutes. Nitroprusside develops a purple color in the presence of acetoacetic acid (and to a much lesser degree, acetone).
- Routine urine testing for ketones (with nitroprusside) is no longer necessary to diagnose DKA.
- Using capillary beta hydroxybutyrate offers a distinct advantage of avoiding unnecessary workup.

10) What can cause a false-negative nitroprusside testing in DKA?
Nitroprusside reacts with acetoacetate and, to a lesser degree, with acetone, but not with beta-hydroxybutyrate. This can cause diagnostic confusion because beta-hydroxybutyrate can become the predominant ketone in severe DKA. The ratio of beta-hydroxybutyrate to acetoacetate is approximately 1:1 in normal subjects and can increase to as high as 10:1 in DKA. This ratio also increases when lactic acidosis coexists with ketoacidosis. It is therefore possible, although unusual, to have a negative serum nitroprusside reaction in the presence of severe ketosis.

11) Can a urine dipstick test for ketones be negative in DKA?
For patients with DKA, the urine dipstick test is highly positive for glucose and ketones. Rarely, urine is negative for ketones because urine dipstick tests can detect only acetoacetate, while the predominant ketone in severe untreated DKA is beta-hydroxybutyrate.

12) What does Ketostix measure in DKA?
Urine dipstick testing with nitroprusside tablets (Acetest) or reagent sticks (Ketostix) measure urine and blood acetone and acetoacetic acid. They do not measure beta-hydroxybutyrate (predominant ketone). Therefore, the patient may appear to have "paradoxical worsening" as beta-hydroxybutyrate is oxidized to acetoacetate in extrahepatic tissues with treatment.

13) What can cause a false-positive urine nitroprusside test?

False-positive nitroprusside urine ketone results can be generated by drugs containing free sulfhydryl groups that react with nitroprusside (eg, captopril, penicillamine, and mesna).

14) Are venous blood samples for biochemical studies sufficiently reliable in the management of DKA?
- Venous blood samples are reliable for the management of critically ill patients with DKA.
    - pH, serum bicarbonate, and potassium are almost similar for arterial and venous samples.
- Venous pH may be used for repeat pH measurements.
    - The slight decrease in pH of venous blood compared to arterial blood (0.03) is not of clinical significance. There is no reason to perform the more painful ABG.

15) How does serum potassium levels change in DKA?
- Serum potassium levels initially are high or normal in patients with DKA. This is due to the extracellular shift of potassium in exchange of hydrogen, which is accumulated in acidosis, in spite of severely depleted total body potassium.
- Serum potassium levels should be checked frequently, as values drop very rapidly with treatment.
- An ECG may be used to assess the cardiac effects of extremes in potassium levels.

16) How does serum sodium levels change in DKA?
- The serum sodium level usually is low.
- The osmotic effect of hyperglycemia moves extravascular water to the intravascular space.
    - For each 100 mg/dL of glucose over 100 mg/dL, the serum sodium level is lowered by approximately 1.6 mEq/L.
    - When glucose levels fall, the serum sodium level rises by a corresponding amount.

17) How will you assess the degree of acidosis in DKA?
- Use bicarbonate levels in conjunction with the anion gap to assess the degree of acidosis that is present. The serum anion gap is calculated as follows:

$$\text{Serum anion gap} = [Na + K] - [Cl + HCO_3]$$

  - It is the actual measured plasma sodium concentration and not the sodium concentration corrected for the simultaneous glucose concentration that is used for this calculation.
- Compensatory hyperventilation reduces the partial pressure of CO_2 and mitigates the fall in arterial pH.

18) What is the expected anion gap in DKA?
- The normal anion gap is 3 to 10 mEq/L.
- Patients with DKA usually present with a serum anion gap greater than 20 mEq/L.
  - > 10 mEq/L - mild cases
  - > 12 mEq/L - moderate and severe cases.

19) What is the cause of the elevated anion gap in DKA?
The elevated anion gap metabolic acidosis is caused by the accumulation of beta-hydroxybutyric and acetoacetic acids.

20) What is the role of plasma osmolarity in the evaluation of DKA?
- Plasma osmolarity usually is increased (greater than 290 mOsm/L) in patients with diabetic ketoacidosis.
- Patients with diabetic ketoacidosis who are in a coma typically have osmolalities greater than 330 mOsm/kg H2O. If the osmolality is less than this in a patient who is comatose, search for another cause of coma.
- If plasma osmolarity cannot be measured directly, it may be calculated with the following formula: plasma osmolarity = 2 (Na + K) + BUN/3 + glucose/18.

21) How will you evaluate treatment response?
- Measure capillary blood ketones to monitor the response to DKA treatment.

- The method of choice is bedside measurement of blood ketones using a ketone meter.
- In the absence of blood ketone measurement, use venous pH and bicarbonate together with bedside blood glucose monitoring to evaluate treatment response.

22) What is the role of ECG in the workup of DKA?
- DKA may be precipitated by a cardiac event.
    - Acute myocardial infarction could be painless in patients with diabetes, particularly in those with autonomic neuropathy.
    - An ECG should be performed every 6 hours during the first day unless the patient is monitored.
- An ECG is a rapid way to assess significant hypokalemia or hyperkalemia.
    - T-wave changes may produce the first warning sign of disturbed serum potassium levels.
        - Low T wave and U wave signify hypokalemia
        - Peaked T waves signify hyperkalemia.

23) What does elevated serum amylase and lipase in DKA mean?
- Acute pancreatitis may precipitate or complicate DKA.
- Serum amylase and lipase are elevated in 20% of patients with DKA who do not have pancreatitis.
    - Therefore, the diagnosis of pancreatitis in patients with DKA and abdominal pain should be based upon clinical findings and imaging.

24) What are the diagnostic problems in DKA?
1. Sodium: whole body sodium is depleted but may appear:
    a. Raised due to dehydration
    b. Normal
    c. Low

2. Potassium: whole body potassium is depleted but may appear:
    a. Raised due to acidosis
    b. Normal
    c. Occasionally low

3. White cell count: Raised in DKA per se and thus not necessarily an indicator of infection.

4. Amylase: Pancreatitis can precipitate DKA, but amylase is raised in the absence of pancreatitis in DKA. Amylase is of salivary origin.

5. Urinary ketones: 3-hydroxybutyrate concentrations in plasma are 2–3 times those of acetoacetate. In acidic states this ratio is increased further. As therapy improves acidosis, levels of acetoacetate rise. Methods that measure only acetoacetate concentration in urine may therefore suggest that ketonemia is worsening.

Management (40)

1) What is the first step in the treatment of DKA?

The first step in the treatment of DKA is infusion of isotonic saline to expand extracellular volume and stabilize cardiovascular status. This also increases insulin responsiveness by lowering the plasma osmolality, reducing vasoconstriction, and improving perfusion, and reducing stress hormone levels.

The next step is correction of the potassium deficit (if present). The choice of fluid replacement should be influenced by the potassium deficit.

2) What is the first priority when treating patients with DKA?
    a. Correction of fluid loss with intravenous fluids
    b. Correction of hyperglycemia with insulin
    c. Correction of acid-base balance
    d. Correction of potassium loss
    e. Treatment of concurrent infection

Ans - a

It is important to pay close attention to the correction of fluid and electrolyte loss during the first hour of treatment. This always should be followed by gradual correction of hyperglycemia and acidosis.

Correction of fluid loss may be sufficient to correct acidosis. The presence of even mild signs of dehydration indicates that at least 3 L of fluid has already been lost.

Start insulin about an hour after IV fluid replacement is started to allow for checking potassium levels. There is little to no advantage in starting insulin prior to rehydration and evaluation of serum potassium levels.

3) How will you manage a case of DKA?

Management of DKA

1. Stabilize the patient's airway, breathing, and circulation.
2. Obtain large bore IV (≥16 gauge) access
    a. Monitor using a cardiac monitor, pulse oximetry, and capnography.
3. Monitor-
    a. serum glucose hourly, and
    b. basic electrolytes and bicarbonate (or venous pH) every two to four hours until the patient is stable.
4. Replete ECF volume and free water deficits
5. Replete potassium deficits
6. Give insulin
7. Determine and treat any underlying cause of DKA (eg, pneumonia or urinary infection, myocardial ischemia).

4) What is the schedule for restoring fluids during treatment of DKA?
- Initial correction of fluid loss is either by isotonic sodium chloride solution or by lactated Ringer solution. The recommended schedule for restoring fluids is as follows:
    - Administer 1-3 L during the first hour.
    - Administer 1 L during the second hour.
    - Administer 1 L during the following 2 hours
    - Administer 1 L every 4 hours, depending on the degree of dehydration and central venous pressure readings

- When the patient becomes euvolemic, switch to half-normal saline at 200-1000 mL/h.
- When blood sugar decreases to less than 180 mg/dL, replace isotonic sodium chloride solution with 5-10% dextrose with half isotonic sodium chloride solution.

5) How will you replete ECF volume and free water deficits in DKA?
The optimal rate of initial isotonic saline infusion is dependent upon the clinical state of the patient:
- Give IV isotonic (0.9%) saline at 1 to 1.5 L per hour for an average-sized adult (ie, 15 to 20 mL/kg per hour), in the absence of cardiac compromise, for the first few hours to hypovolemic patients without shock.
- Give several liters of IV isotonic (0.9%) saline as rapidly as possible to patients with signs of shock.
- After intravascular volume is restored, give one-half isotonic (0.45%) saline at 4 to 14 mL/kg per hour if the corrected serum Na+ is normal or elevated; isotonic saline is continued if the corrected serum Na+ is reduced.
- Add dextrose to the saline solution when the serum glucose reaches 200 mg/dL.

6) When is isotonic saline changed to one-half isotonic saline?
After the second or third hour, the most appropriate IV fluid composition is determined by the sodium concentration "corrected" for the degree of hyperglycemia. To find the "corrected" sodium concentration, add 2 mEq/L to the plasma sodium concentration for each 100 mg/100 mL increase above normal in glucose concentration.

If the "corrected" serum sodium concentration is:
- Less than 135 mEq/L
    - continue isotonic saline at a rate of 250 to 500 mL/hour
- Normal or elevated,
    - switch to one-half isotonic saline at a rate of 250 to 500 mL/hour in order to provide electrolyte-free water

7) How will you correct potassium deficits in DKA?

Regardless of the initial measured serum K+, patients with DKA have a large total body K+ deficit due to urinary losses generated by the glucose osmotic diuresis and secondary hyperaldosteronism. Despite the total body potassium deficit, the serum potassium concentration is usually normal (in 60%) or elevated (in 35%) at presentation. This is largely due to insulin deficiency and hyperosmolality, each of which cause potassium movement out of the cells.

- If initial serum K+ is below 3.3 mEq/L
    - Hold insulin
    - Give potassium chloride 20 to 40 mEq/hour IV until K+ concentration is above 3.3 mEq/L (20 to 40 mEq/L added to saline).
- If initial serum K+ is between 3.3 and 5.3 mEq/L
    - Give potassium chloride 20 to 30 mEq per liter IV fluid
    - Maintain serum K+ between 4 to 5 mEq/L.
- If initial serum K+ is above 5.3 mEq/L
    - Do not give potassium
    - Check serum K+ every 2 hours
    - Delay administration of potassium chloride until serum K+ has fallen to 5 to 5.2 mEq/L.

8) How does administration of insulin affect potassium level?

Insulin stimulates the entry of potassium into cells and can cause a dramatic fall in the serum potassium concentration, despite potassium replacement.

9) How will you initiate insulin therapy in DKA?
- Use low-dose insulin regimen
    - It does not induce severe hypoglycemia or hypokalemia that may be observed with a high-dose insulin regimen.
- Use only IV regular insulin or rapid-acting insulin analogs for correction of hyperglycemia.
    - Regular insulin is preferred due to its much lower cost.
- Intravenous route is preferable

- Subcutaneous absorption of insulin is reduced in DKA because of dehydration.
- Subcutaneous insulin analog (aspart) may be used in mild cases.

10) How will you give insulin in DKA?
- Do not give insulin if initial serum K+ is below 3.3 mEq/L; replete K+ and fluid deficit first.
    - Insulin will worsen the hypokalemia by driving potassium into the cells, and this could trigger cardiac arrhythmias, cardiac arrest, and respiratory muscle weakness.
- Give all patients with a serum K+ > 3.3 mEq/L regular insulin.
    - Either of two regimens can be used:
        - start a continuous IV infusion at a rate of 0.14 units/kg per hour without a bolus dose: **OR**
        - 0.1 units/kg IV bolus, then start a continuous IV infusion at 0.1 units/kg per hour.
- If serum glucose does not fall by at least 50 to 70 mg/dL in the first hour, double the rate of insulin infusion.
- When the serum glucose reaches 200 mg/dL, it may be possible to decrease the infusion rate to 0.02 to 0.05 units/kg per hour.
- Continue insulin infusion until ketoacidosis is resolved, serum glucose is below 200 mg/dL, and subcutaneous insulin is begun.

11) What is the initial insulin dose for DKA?
- IV bolus of regular insulin (0.1 units/kg body weight)
- Followed within five minutes by a continuous IV insulin infusion using an infusion pump, if available, at a rate of 0.1 U/kg/h.
    - Infuse 24 units of regular insulin in 60 mL of isotonic sodium chloride solution at a rate of 15 mL/h (6 U/h) until the blood glucose level drops to less than 200 mg/dL.
    - Decrease the rate of infusion to 5-7.5 mL/h (2-3 U/h) until the ketoacidotic state abates.
- In the absence of an IV infusion pump use 60 U of insulin in 500 mL of isotonic sodium chloride solution at a rate of 50 mL/h.

These doses of IV regular insulin decrease the serum glucose concentration by 50 to 70 mg/dL per hour. Higher doses do not generally produce a more prominent glucose-lowering effect, because the insulin receptors are fully saturated and activated by the lower doses. However, if the serum glucose does not fall by at least 50 to 70 mg/dL from the initial value in the first hour, the insulin infusion rate should be doubled every hour until a steady decline in serum glucose of this magnitude is achieved.

12) What is the indication for delaying the initiation of insulin therapy in DKA?
    - The only indication for delaying the initiation of insulin therapy is:
        o if the serum potassium is below 3.3 mEq/L
            - Insulin will worsen hypokalemia by driving potassium into the cells.
    - Patients with an initial serum potassium below 3.3 mEq/L should receive fluid and potassium replacement prior to treatment with insulin.

13) What are the advantages of rapid-acting insulin analogs over regular insulin in DKA?

There is no advantage of rapid-acting insulin analogs over regular insulin. Intravenous regular insulin and glulisine insulin are equally effective and equipotent for the treatment of DKA.

14) What is the role for long- or intermediate-acting insulin in the management of DKA?

    Acute management of DKA
    - For acute management of DKA, there is no role for long- or intermediate-acting insulin.
    - In patients with mild DKA (particularly in patients with mild DKA due to reduced or missed doses of basal insulin), intermediate- or long-acting insulin can be administered at the initiation of treatment, along with rapid-acting insulin.
    - Patients with mild DKA can be safely treated with subcutaneous, rapid-acting insulin analogs.

    After recovery from ketoacidosis

- Long-acting (glargine, detemir) or intermediate-acting (NPH) insulin is administered after recovery from ketoacidosis, prior to discontinuation of IV insulin. This is to ensure that adequate insulin is available when IV insulin is discontinued.
    - In this setting, do not use degludec, because of its 25-hour half-life and 42-hour duration of effect; it will take at least three to four days to reach a steady state.

15) How does insulin therapy lower the serum glucose concentration in DKA?
    a. By decreasing hepatic glucose production
    b. By enhancing peripheral utilization
    c. By decreasing lipolysis
    d. By decreasing glucagon secretion
    e. By increasing ketone utilization

Ans – a
- The major effect by which Insulin lowers the serum glucose concentration is by decreasing hepatic glucose production.
- Enhancing peripheral utilization is a less important effect.
- Insulin diminishes ketone production by reducing both lipolysis and glucagon secretion and may augment ketone utilization.
    - Inhibition of lipolysis requires a much lower level of insulin than that required to reduce the serum glucose concentration. Therefore, if the administered dose of insulin is reducing the glucose concentration, it should be more than enough to stop ketone generation.

16) How much can volume repletion alone reduce serum glucose initially?

Volume repletion alone can initially reduce the serum glucose by 35 to 70 mg/dL per hour due to:
- ECF expansion,
- reduction of plasma osmolality,
- increased urinary losses resulting from improved renal perfusion and glomerular filtration, and
- reduction in the levels of "stress hormones".

17) What is the optimal rate of glucose decline in DKA?
- The optimal rate of glucose decline is 100 mg/dL/h.
- Do not allow the blood glucose level to fall below 200 mg/dL during the first 4-5 hours of treatment.
    o Hypoglycemia may develop rapidly with correction of ketoacidosis due to improved insulin sensitivity.
- Allowing blood glucose to drop to hypoglycemic levels is a common mistake that usually results in a rebound ketosis derived by counter-regulatory hormones.
- Rapid correction of hyperglycemia and hyperosmolarity may shift water rapidly to the hyperosmolar intracellular space and may induce cerebral edema.

18) Should insulin therapy begin before hypokalemia is treated in DKA?

Rehydration and insulin treatment directly facilitates potassium reentry into the cell and may precipitate dangerous hypokalemia. Therefore, in severe hypokalemia, do not start insulin therapy unless potassium replacement is started; this is to avoid potentially serious cardiac dysrhythmia that may result from hypokalemia.

19) When is potassium chloride administered in the treatment of DKA?
- If the potassium level is greater than 6 mEq/L, do not administer a potassium supplement.
- If the potassium level is 4.5 - 6 mEq/L, administer 10 mEq/h of potassium chloride.
- If the potassium level is 3 - 4.5 mEq/L, administer 20 mEq/h of potassium chloride.

20) When should potassium replacement be initiated in DKA?
- Potassium replacement should be started with initial fluid replacement if potassium levels are normal or low.

- Add 20-40 mEq/L of potassium chloride to each liter of fluid once the potassium level is less than 5.5 mEq/L.
- Potassium can be given as follows: two thirds as KCl, one third as KPO4.

21) How often should serum potassium levels be monitored in the treatment of DKA?
- Monitor serum potassium levels hourly, and the infusion must be stopped if the potassium level is greater than 5 mEq/L.
- The monitoring of serum potassium must continue even after potassium infusion is stopped in the case of recurrence of hypokalemia.

22) How is acidosis treated in DKA?
- Bicarbonate is not usually given as acidosis will improve with fluids and insulin.
- Rapid and early correction of acidosis with sodium bicarbonate may worsen hypokalemia and cause paradoxical cellular acidosis.
- Sodium bicarbonate is infused only if decompensated acidosis starts to threaten the patient's life, especially when associated with either sepsis or lactic acidosis.
- If sodium bicarbonate is indicated, 100-150 mL of 1.4% concentration is infused initially. This may be repeated every half hour if necessary.

23) When is sodium bicarbonate indicated in DKA?
1. Patients with an arterial pH ≤6.9 in whom decreased cardiac contractility and vasodilatation can impair tissue perfusion. At an arterial pH above 7.0, bicarbonate therapy is not necessary since therapy with insulin and volume expansion will largely reverse the metabolic acidosis.
    a. For patients with pH ≤6.9, give 100 mEq of sodium bicarbonate in 400 mL sterile water administered over two hours.
    b. If the serum potassium is less than 5.3 mEq/L, add 20 mEq of KCl.

i. When the bicarbonate concentration increases, the serum potassium may fall and more aggressive KCl replacement may be required.

2. Patients with potentially life-threatening hyperkalemia
   a. Bicarbonate administration in academic patients may drive potassium into cells, thereby lowering the serum potassium concentration.
   b. Administer sodium bicarbonate if the potassium level is > 6.4 mEq/L.

Monitor the venous pH and bicarbonate concentration every two hours, and bicarbonate doses can be repeated until the pH rises above 7.0.

24) What are the indications for phosphate replacement in DKA?
- Whole-body phosphate depletion is common in uncontrolled diabetes mellitus, but the serum phosphate concentration may initially be normal or elevated due to movement of phosphate out of the cells. Similar to potassium, phosphate depletion and hypophosphatemia may be rapidly unmasked following the institution of insulin therapy and IV volume expansion. This frequently leads to asymptomatic hypophosphatemia, which gradually resolves.
- When the patient stabilizes, phosphate-rich food such as dairy products and almonds may be recommended.
- The routine use of phosphate replacement in the treatment of DKA is not recommended.
    o Phosphate replacement may have adverse effects, such as hypocalcemia and hypomagnesemia
- Phosphate replacement should be strongly considered if severe hypophosphatemia occurs (serum phosphate concentration below 1 mg/dL), especially if cardiac dysfunction, hemolytic anemia, and/or respiratory depression develop.
    o When needed, potassium or sodium phosphate 20 to 30 mEq can be added to 1 L of IV fluid.

25) Which patients are primarily affected by cerebral edema during treatment of DKA?
- Cerebral edema is a serious, major complication that may evolve at any time during treatment and primarily affects children (1%) with DKA.
  - Almost all affected patients are younger than 20 years old
  - It is the leading cause of DKA mortality in children.
- Deterioration of the level of consciousness in spite of improved metabolic state usually indicates the occurrence of cerebral edema.
- MRI is used to confirm the diagnosis.

26) What are the diagnostic features of cerebral edema in DKA?
- Headache is the earliest clinical manifestation, followed by decreased arousal.
- Fluctuating level of consciousness
- Abnormal central nervous system respiratory patterns
- Incontinence
- Elevated diastolic blood pressure
- Bradycardia
- Seizures
- Pupillary changes.

27) How is cerebral edema managed in DKA?
- Cerebral edema that occurs at initiation of therapy tends to worsen during the course of treatment.
- 0.5-1 g/kg intravenous mannitol may be given over the course of 20 minutes and repeated if no response is seen in 30-120 minutes.
- If no response to mannitol occurs, hypertonic saline (3%) may be given at 5-10 mg/kg over the course of 30 minutes.

28) How is myocardial injury treated in DKA?
Nonspecific myocardial injury may occur in severe DKA; it is associated with minute elevations of troponin T and CK-MB) and initial ECG changes compatible with myocardial infarction.

Acidosis and very high levels of free fatty acids could cause membrane instability and biomarker leakage. Coronary arteriography usually is normal, and patients tend to recover fully without further evidence of ischemic heart disease. Regardless of the pathogenesis, the presence of minute biomarker elevations and ECG changes do not necessarily signify MI in DKA.

29) How do you monitor response to treatment of DKA?
- Serum glucose
  - Every hour until stable
- Serum electrolytes, BUN, creatinine, and venous pH
  - Every two to four hours, depending upon disease severity and the clinical response.

30) Not used for monitoring resolution of DKA
   a. Capillary beta-hydroxybutyrate
   b. Venous pH
   c. Bicarbonate level
   d. Serum ketone levels by the nitroprusside method

Ans - d

- Correction of the ketoacidosis can be monitored by direct measurement of serum or capillary beta-hydroxybutyrate. In the absence of blood ketone measurement, use venous pH and bicarbonate together with bedside blood glucose monitoring to evaluate treatment response.
- Assessments of urinary or serum ketone levels by the nitroprusside method can be used for the initial diagnosis of ketoacidosis; it should not be used for monitoring resolution of DKA.
  - Nitroprusside reacts mainly with acetoacetate, to a much lesser degree with acetone; it does not react with beta-hydroxybutyrate.
  - A positive nitroprusside test may persist for up to 36 hours after resolution of the ketoacidosis due to a positive reaction with acetone, which is slowly eliminated, mainly via the lungs.
  - Acetone is not an acid. Therefore, a persistent nitroprusside reaction due to acetone does not indicate ketoacidosis.

- Treatment of ketoacidosis shifts the reaction between beta-hydroxybutyrate and acetoacetate toward acetoacetate. This may result in an increasingly positive nitroprusside test (due to higher acetoacetate concentrations) despite an overall improvement of ketoacidosis.

31) Is monitoring with arterial blood gases necessary during the treatment of DKA?

Monitoring with arterial blood gases is unnecessary during the treatment of DKA; venous pH, which is approximately 0.03 units lower than arterial pH, is adequate to assess the response to therapy.

32) What is the alternative to monitoring venous pH?

An alternative to monitoring venous pH is to monitor the serum bicarbonate concentration (to assess correction of the metabolic acidosis) and the serum anion gap (to assess correction of the ketoacidemia).

33) What is the role of anion gap in the management of DKA?

The anion gap is an estimate of the sum of beta-hydroxybutyrate and acetoacetate in the serum. The anion gap returns to the normal range when ketoacid anions (beta-hydroxybutyrate and acetoacetate) have disappeared from the serum.

34) What is the alternative to monitoring anion gap?

An alternative to the measurement of anion gap is to measure capillary blood beta-hydroxybutyrate every two hours using bedside ketone meters.

35) Is monitoring capillary blood beta-hydroxybutyrate necessary during the treatment of DKA?

Capillary blood beta-hydroxybutyrate may be measured every two hours using bedside ketone meters as an alternative to the measurement of anion gap. When bedside meters are not available, monitoring venous pH and/or the venous bicarbonate and anion gap is sufficient.

36) Why do almost all patients develop a normal anion gap acidosis during the resolution phase of the ketoacidosis?

In the absence of severe kidney disease, almost all patients develop a normal anion gap acidosis ("non-gap" or "hyperchloremic acidosis") during the resolution phase of the ketoacidosis. This occurs because aggressive IV volume expansion reverses volume contraction and improves renal function, which accelerates the loss of ketoacid anions with sodium and potassium. The loss of these ketoacid anion salts into the urine represent "potential" bicarbonate loss from the body. Insulin therapy will have no further effect on the acidosis when this stage evolves. The hyperchloremic acidosis will slowly resolve as the kidneys excrete ammonium chloride and regenerate bicarbonate.

37) Which are the two most common complications of the treatment of DKA?

Hypoglycemia and hypokalemia are the most common complications of the treatment of DKA.

38) How do you decide whether DKA has been resolved?

The DKA is considered to be resolved when the following goals are reached:
- The ketoacidosis has resolved
    - Normalization of the serum anion gap (less than 12 mEq/L)
    - Normal blood beta-hydroxybutyrate levels, when available.
- The patient is able to eat

The correction of the ketoacidosis can be determined by measuring:
- Venous pH, and/or
- Serum electrolytes and bicarbonate concentrations with calculation of the serum anion gap.
- Beta-hydroxybutyrate directly.

39) When can patients with DKA be discharged from the hospital?

When the condition is stable, pH exceeds 7.3, and bicarbonate is greater than 18 mEq/L, the patient can eat a meal preceded by a subcutaneous dose of regular insulin.

40) How will you manage the transition from IV insulin to subcutaneous insulin?
- Continue the IV insulin infusion till the patient is able to eat.
- Initiate a multiple-dose (basal-bolus), subcutaneous insulin schedule when the ketoacidosis has resolved, and the patient is able to eat.
    - The most convenient time to transition to subcutaneous insulin is before a meal.
- Continue the IV insulin infusion for two to four hours after initiating the short- or rapid-acting subcutaneous insulin.
    - Abrupt discontinuation of IV insulin acutely reduces insulin levels and may result in recurrence of hyperglycemia and/or ketoacidosis.
- Basal insulin (NPH, glargine, or detemir) can be administered either (a) at the same time as the first injection of rapid-acting insulin, or (b) earlier (for example, the previous evening), along with a decrease in the rate of IV insulin infusion.

HYPEROSMOLAR HYPERGLYCEMIC STATE (HHS) (15)

1) What is HHS?
- HHS is characterized by hyperglycemia, hyperosmolarity, and dehydration without significant ketoacidosis.
    - The serum glucose concentration in HHS frequently exceeds 1000 mg/dL
    - In DKA, serum glucose concentration is below 800 mg/dL and often in the 350 to 450 mg/dL
- Most patients present with severe dehydration and focal or global neurologic deficits.
- HHS and DKA are observed simultaneously (overlap cases) in up to one third of cases.
- HHS most commonly develops in individuals older than 65 years (DKA is more common in individuals <65 years).

Typical laboratory characteristics of DKA and HHS

	DKA			HHS
	Mild	**Moderate**	**Severe**	
Plasma glucose (mg/dL)	>250	>250	>250	>600
Arterial pH	7.25 to 7.30	7.00 to 7.24	<7.00	>7.30
Serum bicarbonate (mEq/L)	15 to 18	10 to <15	<10	>18
Urine ketones	Positive	Positive	Positive	Small
Serum ketones - Nitroprusside reaction	Positive	Positive	Positive	≤ Small
Serum ketones - Enzymatic assay of beta hydroxybutyrate (normal range <0.6 mmol/L)	3 to 4 mmol/L	4 to 8 mmol/L	>8 mmol/L	<0.6 mmol/L
Effective serum osmolality (mOsm/kg)◊	Variable	Variable	Variable	>320
Anion gap§	>10	>12	>12	Variable
Alteration in sensoria	Alert	Alert/drowsy	Stupor/coma	Stupor/coma

◊ Calculation: 2[measured Na (mEq/L)] + glucose (mg/dL)/18.

§ Calculation: (Na+) − (Cl− + HCO3−) (mEq/L).

2) What is the underlying mechanism of HHS?
   - The basic underlying mechanism of HHS is a relative reduction in effective circulating insulin with a concomitant rise in counterregulatory hormones (glucagon, epinephrine, growth hormone, and cortisol).
     o The levels of these hormones increase during an acute illness (eg, major infections, myocardial infarction, or pancreatitis) or stress.
   - Unlike patients with DKA, most patients with HHS do not develop significant ketoacidosis.
     o Insulin remains available in amounts sufficient to inhibit lipolysis and ketogenesis but insufficient to prevent hyperglycemia.

3) How does HHS present?
   - Symptoms of HHS develop insidiously with polyuria, polydipsia, and weight loss, often persisting for several days before hospital admission.
     o In contrast, DKA usually evolves rapidly, over a 24-hour period.
   - Neurologic symptoms are common in HHS.
     o Lethargy
     o Focal signs (hemiparesis or hemianopsia)
     o Seizures
     o Obtundation
     o Coma in later stages.
   - Neurologic deterioration primarily occurs in patients with an effective plasma osmolality above 320 to 330 mosmol/kg.

4) How does DKA and HHS differ clinically?
   - DKA
     o Metabolic acidosis is often the major finding
     o Serum glucose concentration is often in the 350 to 500 mg/dL (below 800 mg/dL).
   - HHS

- There is little or no metabolic acidosis (ie, ketoacid accumulation)
- Serum glucose concentration frequently exceeds 1000 mg/dL
- Plasma osmolality may reach 380 mOsmol/kg
- Neurologic abnormalities are frequently present (including coma in 25 to 50 percent of cases).

5) What are the diagnostic features of HHS?

Diagnostic features of HHS include the following:
- Plasma glucose level of 600 mg/dL or greater
- Effective serum osmolality of 320 mOsm/kg or greater
- Profound dehydration, up to an average of 9L
- Serum pH greater than 7.30
- Bicarbonate concentration greater than 15 mEq/L
- Small ketonuria and low to absent ketonemia
- Some alteration in consciousness

6) How much is the free water loss in HHS?

Typical free water loss in DKA is approximately 9 liters (100 to 200 mL/kg of body weight).

Typical total body deficits of water and electrolytes in HHS

	DKA	HHS
Total water (L)	6	9
Water (mL/kg)	100	100 to 200
Na⁺ (mEq/kg)	7 to 10	5 to 13
Cl⁻ (mEq/kg)	3 to 5	5 to 15
K⁺ (mEq/kg)	3 to 5	4 to 6

PO$_4$ (mmol/kg)	5 to 7	3 to 7
Mg^{++} (mEq/kg)	1 to 2	1 to 2
Ca^{++} (mEq/kg)	1 to 2	1 to 2

7) Why is ketosis absent in HHS?
   - Insulin, in very small doses, can suppress lipolysis and ketogenesis, but cannot inhibit gluconeogenesis.
     o The concentration of insulin required to suppress lipolysis is only one-tenth that required to inhibit gluconeogenesis (ie, promote glucose utilization).
   - Insulin deficiency in HHS is less severe compared with DKA.
     o This much insulin is enough to minimize lipolysis (and therefore ketoacid formation) but is not enough to block gluconeogenesis, and thereby prevent hyperglycemia.

8) What causes the hyperosmolarity in HHS?
   - Plasma osmolality is always elevated in patients with HHS but less so with DKA.
     o Hyperglycemia raises the ECF osmolality and shifts water from the ICF space to the ECF space. Expansion of the ECF dilutes serum sodium and reduces its concentration.
   - Glucosuria generates an osmotic diuresis which causes the excretion of sodium and potassium salts, and water.
     o Osmotic diuresis causes a decrease in total body water.
       ▪ Up to 9L of water deficit can develop.
   - If the renal water loss is not compensated for by oral water intake, dehydration leads to hypovolemia.
   - In an insulinopenic state, hyperglycemia is exacerbated by continued gluconeogenesis and inability to clear glucose.

9) How does hyperglycemia affect serum sodium concentration?
   - The serum sodium concentration falls between 1.6 and 2.4 mEq/L for each 100 mg/100 mL increase in glucose.

- Use of a simple ratio of a 2 mEq/L decline in sodium for each 100 mg/100 mL increase in glucose concentration above the normal range is good practice.

10) What does an elevated serum Na concentration mean in HHS?
   - Most patients with HHS are mildly hyponatremic.
     - However, patients with HHS who have a marked osmotic diuresis may present with a normal or even elevated serum Na concentration, despite a markedly elevated serum glucose concentration that can exceed 1000 mg/dL.
   - These patients have a markedly elevated effective osmolality and often have neurologic symptoms that can include seizures and coma.
     - Inadequate water intake contributes to the hyperosmolality.
     - This is a particular problem in hot weather and in older individuals who may have an impaired thirst mechanism.

11) Which patients are most likely to develop hyperosmolar hyperglycemic state (HHS)?
   - HHS most commonly occurs in patients with type 2 DM who have some concomitant illness that leads to reduced fluid intake.
   - The most at-risk population consists of the elderly or chronically ill.
     - The average age of patients with HHS is 60 years.
   - An infection (pneumonia, urinary tract infection) is the single most common cause.
   - Any living situation or comorbidity that prevent adequate hydration place these patients at risk
     - immobility,
     - advanced age,
     - debility,
     - dementia,
     - impaired thirst response,
     - restricted access to water.

12) What are the precipitating causes of HHS?

Infection is the most common preceding illness. Stroke or myocardial infarction can also cause HHS. Consider MI in all patients with HHS until it is excluded.

Precipitating factors for HHS

---

1. Inadequate insulin treatment or noncompliance (20 to 40 %)
2. Acute illness
3. Infection (30 to 60 %)
    a. Pneumonia
    b. Urinary tract infection
    c. Sepsis
4. Cerebral vascular accident
5. Myocardial infarction
6. Acute pancreatitis
7. Acute pulmonary embolism
8. Intestinal obstruction
9. Dialysis, peritoneal
10. Mesenteric thrombosis
11. Renal failure
12. Heat stroke
13. Hypothermia
14. Subdural hematoma
15. Severe burns
16. Endocrine
    a. Acromegaly
    b. Thyrotoxicosis
    c. Cushing's syndrome
17. Drugs/therapy
    a. Beta-adrenergic blockers
    b. Calcium-channel blockers
    c. Chlorpromazine
    d. Steroids
    e. Thiazide diuretics
    f. Total parenteral nutrition
18. Previously undiagnosed diabetes

13) How do you decide whether HHS has resolved?

The HHS is considered to be resolved when the following goals are reached:
- Patients are mentally alert
- Effective plasma osmolality has fallen below 315 mOsmol/kg
- The patient is able to eat.

14) How will you manage the transition from IV insulin to subcutaneous insulin?

IV insulin infusion can be tapered and a multiple-dose (basal-bolus), subcutaneous insulin schedule started when the serum glucose falls below 250 to 300 mg/dL.

15) What is the mortality rate for HHS?
- The overall mortality for HHS is 5-20%. The mortality rate of DKA is about 1-5%.
- Mortality in hyperglycemic crises is primarily due to the underlying precipitating illness and only rarely to the metabolic complications of hyperglycemia or ketoacidosis.
- The prognosis of hyperglycemic crisis is substantially worse at the extremes of age and in the presence of coma and hypotension.